MAY 03
2/08 -11

GLEN ELLYN PUBLIC LIBRARY

3 1322 00388 2157

EVENTS & OUTCOMES
THE
RUSSIAN
REVOLUTION

STEWART ROSS

GLEN ELLYN PUBLIC LIBRARY
400 DUANE STREET
GLEN ELLYN, ILLINOIS 60137

RAINTREE
STECK-VAUGHN
PUBLISHERS

A Harcourt Company

Austin   New York
www.raintreesteckvaughn.com

First published 2003 by Raintree Steck-Vaughn
Publishers, an imprint of Steck-Vaughn Company

© Evans Brothers Limited 2002

All rights reserved. No part of this book may be
reproduced or utilized in any form or by any
means, electronic or mechanical, including photo-
copying, recording, or by any information storage
and retrieval system, without permission in writing
from the Publishers. Inquiries should be addressed
to: Copyright Permissions, Steck-Vaughn Company,
P.O. Box 26015, Austin, TX 78755.

Library of Congress Cataloging-in-Publication Data is
available upon request

ISBN 0-7398-5801-7

Printed in Spain. Bound in the United States.

1 2 3 4 5 6 7 8 9 0 LB 05 04 03 02

Edited by Rachel Norridge
Designed by Neil Sayer
Consultant: Professor Eric Hopkins

Acknowledgments

Cover image: Hulton Getty **contents page:** David King Collection **p. 6** the art archive **p. 7** Topham Picturepoint **p. 8** Hulton Getty **p. 9** David King Collection **p. 11** David King Collection **p. 12** (top) Novosti (bottom) David King Collection **p. 13** Topham Picturepoint **p. 14** Novosti **p. 15** (top) David King Collection (bottom) Novosti **p. 16** Novosti **p. 17** David King Collection **p. 18** Novosti **p. 19** David King Collection **p. 20** David King Collection **p. 21** David King Collection **p. 22** David King Collection **p. 23** David King Collection **p. 24** David King Collection **p. 25** David King Collection **p. 26** David King Collection **p. 27** David King Collection **p. 28** Novosti **p. 29** David King Collection **p. 30** (top) David King Collection (bottom) Hulton Getty **p. 31** (inset) Novosti (bottom) David King Collection **p. 32** David King Collection **p. 33** (top) Novosti (bottom) Hulton Getty **p. 34** David King Collection **p. 35** David King Collection **p. 36** Novosti **p. 37** Topham Picturepoint **p. 38** David King Collection **p. 39** Novosti **p. 40** (top) Novosti (bottom) David King Collection **p. 41** Novosti **p. 42** David King Collection **p. 43** David King Collection **p. 44** David King Collection **p. 45** David King Collection **p. 46** Novosti **p. 47** David King Collection **p. 48** David King Collection **p. 49** (top) Novosti (bottom) David King Collection **p. 50** David King Collection **p. 51** David King Collection **p. 52** David King Collection **p. 53** David King Collection **p. 54** David King Collection **p. 55** (top) Novosti (bottom) Hulton Getty **p. 56** Novosti **p. 58** David King Collection **p. 59** (top) Novosti (bottom) Hulton Getty **p. 61** (top) David King Collection (bottom) Hulton Getty **p. 62** David King Collection **p. 63** David King Collection **p. 64** (top) Topham Picturepoint (bottom) Hulton Getty **p. 65** Hulton Getty **p. 67** Topham Picturepoint **p. 68** David King Collection **p. 69** Topham Picturepoint **p. 70** Topham Picturepoint **p. 71** Topham Picturepoint **p. 72** David King Collection

CONTENTS

INTRODUCTION

The storming of the Bastille, Paris, 1789, marked the beginning of the French Revolution. It established the tradition of revolutionary violence inherited by Russian radicals of the 19th and 20th centuries.

The Russian Revolution, in the words of the American journalist John Reed, "shook the world." The collapse of Europe's last empire that ruled with absolute and unrestricted power, and its replacement by an authoritarian communist (or, more specifically, Marxist) regime, was one of the most significant events of modern times. It was certainly a defining moment in the history of the 20th century. The Russian Revolution was greater in scale and scope than either of its two great 18th-century predecessors—it was more radical than the American Revolution and arguably more complete and enduring than the French Revolution. Indeed, for 70 years at the least, it redefined our very understanding of the word "revolution."

Worldwide Impact

Within the old Russian Empire, reborn (more or less) as the Union of Soviet Socialist Republics (USSR), the Revolution accelerated changes already in progress and introduced new ones. It speeded up the process by which a primarily agricultural, peasant society was transformed into an industrial and technological one, capable of overcoming the Nazi onslaught in World War II and, for a time, leading the United States in the post-war space race. Rapid economic development certainly would have occurred in Russia, but the Revolution determined its pace and nature.

Outside Russia, the first consequence of the Revolution was Russia's withdrawal from World War I. In the longer term, it set the USSR outside the dominant bloc of capitalist liberal democracies. At the same time, it offered an apparently democratic (in name) and viable alternative to the form of government dominant in the West after World War I. This was, through the European empires, the suggested role model for the rest of the world. Communism, up to this time scorned as unrealistic and impractical, now had to be taken seriously. Moreover, its theoretical underpinning—Marxism (see page 72)—became a recognized philosophical tool for interpreting the past, judging the present, and predicting the future.

Italian fascists hold up portraits of their communist opponents. The fear of communism spreading west from Russia led to the emergence in Europe of right-wing, anti-communist movements, of which fascism was the most prominent.

Politics Redefined

For 70 years, various radical left-wing groups, inspired and sometimes supported by the Soviets, provided vigorous opposition to existing governments. In some countries, most notably China in 1949, they succeeded in gaining power.

Elsewhere, in order to head off the perceived communist threat, governments found it appropriate to introduce socialist-style policies of their own. At one time or another, most Western democracies, even the United States, stepped up their efforts to alleviate the ill effects of unregulated capitalism.

Anti-communist sentiment played an important part in spawning German and Italian fascism. The very name of the German fascist party, the National Socialists (Nazis), was a tribute to the appeal of its left-wing opponents. In short, the events of 1917–1924 redefined practical politics and established an ideological divide on a scale not seen since the Reformation, or even since the great religious clashes of the period between 500 and 1000 A.D.

NOTE: DATES AND NAMES

At the end of January 1918, Russia switched from the Julian calendar to the Gregorian calendar commonly used in the West. All dates before the change are given in the old Julian calendar, which was 13 days behind. Names are given in their most common form—for example, "V. I. Lenin" instead of "Vladimir Lenin," and endings as "-ov" instead of "-off."

A women's battalion guarding the Winter Palace, Petrograd, in 1917. The Soviet regime heralded female emancipation but rarely permitted women to rise to positions of major importance.

A lonely end—the captive Nicholas II in 1917.

Contrasting Views

Before 1953, professional historians in the West largely shunned the Russian Revolution because they were denied access to Soviet archives. Soviet historians were confined to analysis that supported the party line. This meant emphasizing that the events of 1917–1921 marked a complete break with the past. It also meant praising the leadership of Lenin and Stalin for sensing and then harnessing the wishes of the people.

In the West, the popular pre-1953 view of the Revolution (at least in anti-communist circles) was that a popular movement overthrew the tsarist regime and was then hijacked by a band of dedicated, yet unrepresentative, revolutionaries who used it to further their own fanatical ends. The participation of non-Russians, women, and the masses outside Petrograd (St. Petersburg) and Moscow was largely ignored. The incompetent Tsar Nicholas II and his wife Alexandra were often portrayed as innocent, almost saintly victims.

New Perspectives

The collapse of the USSR in 1991 suddenly put the Revolution in a different perspective. It was no longer seen as ushering in the modern age. Instead, it marked the start of a limited era, Russia's 74-year "communist phase." The Russians themselves tended to view the events of 1917–1991 as an unwelcome detour, best forgotten. Non-Russian historians, able to study material long denied them, started the lengthy process of providing a fresh analysis.

A May Day workers' demonstration, Petrograd, 1917. The Provisional Government, which had replaced the tsarist regime earlier in the year, had failed to fulfill working class hopes for peace and prosperity.

Although the work is far from complete, interesting conclusions have begun to emerge. Two of them are worth noting here. First, popular support for the Revolution seems to have been more widespread than previously thought. Second, although events in Petrograd and Moscow were crucial, the rest of the tsarist empire also played an important role.

When Was the Revolution?

There is little agreement about the timing and nature of the Russian Revolution. Traditionally, historians spoke of two revolutions in 1917: the first (in February) establishing the Provisional Government and the second (in October) being the Bolshevik takeover. Now, a number of historians argue that it is best to regard the two changes of government in 1917 as part of the same process.

In addition, just as the expression "French Revolution" covers the events of (at least) 1789–1795 and embraces various regimes, there is a tendency to broaden the scope of the term "Russian Revolution." There is widespread disagreement over when the Revolution ended. The traditional dates are either 1921 (the end of the Civil War) or 1924 (the death of Lenin and the date chosen for this book). Others believe the Revolution continued until the end of Stalin's first Five-Year Plan in 1932 or even until he completed his great purges in 1938, over 20 years after the collapse of the tsarist regime.

CHAPTER ONE

THE TSAR AND HIS PEOPLE

The Empire

The Russian Empire covered approximately one-sixth of the Earth's land surface. At its greatest extent it stretched nearly 5,000 miles (8,000 km) east-west and nearly 2,000 miles (3,200 km) north-south. Size did not automatically signify wealth, however; more than 92 percent of this territory was unsuitable for agriculture.

In 1897, the Empire's population was 124 million and growing fast; by 1914, it had topped 170 million. Although we speak of the Empire as "Russian," less than half of its peoples were Russians (55.6 million in 1897). The rest included 22.4 million Ukrainians, 7.9 million Poles, 5.9 million Belorussians (or "White Russians"), 5 million Jews, 3.1 million Finns, and more than one million each of other national groups, including Germans, Caucasians, and Turkic Muslims. All minorities were subject to Russification: a haphazard campaign to spread the Russian language and culture.

The Russian Empire, 1900

Sons of the soil—peasant farmers at work at the end of the 19th century.

Tsar Alexander III (1881–1894), who presided over a fiercely reactionary regime of counter-reform and Russification.

Classes

The great majority of people (some 85 percent in 1900) were peasants. They lived in self-governing village communities, known as *mir*. The Russian peasants had a long history of violent rebellion, most notably in the Pugachev Rebellion of 1773–1775. In 1900, the most common peasant grievance was discontent with the terms of the 1861 Emancipation Edict. This had freed them from serfdom but granted them only half the land that they believed was all theirs by right.

The rest of the population was made up of the privileged nobility, priests of the Russian Orthodox Church, a small but rapidly growing industrial working class, and an equally small but more diverse middle class. These last groups were largely urban (see pages 14–15).

The Autocracy

The government was in the hands of an autocratic (unrestricted) tsar, supposedly appointed by God. Before 1905 his power was, in theory, absolute. He had supreme and unlimited power in all matters except Church ones. Many, like Prime Minister Sergei Witte in 1906, believed this was the only way the empire could be governed:

... if the Tsar's government fails, you will see absolute chaos in Russia, and it will be many a year before you see another government able to control the ... Russian nation.

In practice, the tsar had little impact on the day-to-day lives of his people. The sheer size of his empire, coupled with extremes of weather, the inefficiency of the bureaucracy, and poor communications, meant that most decisions were made at province, district, or even village level.

Nicholas and Alexandra

Nicholas II, Russia's last tsar (ruled 1894–1917), was a quiet, unimaginative man. He had limited ability and took little interest in the complexities of government. He lacked the judgment and confidence to support consistently those who might have helped him. Most damaging of all, he was tiresomely stubborn, particularly in his belief that God had appointed him to his position of autocratic supremacy.

Tsaritsa Alexandra (1872–1918), Nicholas' German-born wife, was as out of touch with popular sentiment as her husband. She was passionately devoted to Nicholas and to his autocracy, telling him:

Never forget you are and must remain authocratic [sic] emperor.

She was equally devoted to their large family, particularly her hemophiliac eldest son, the tsarevitch Alexis. Her close involvement with the notorious philanderer and supposed holy man Gregory Rasputin (1872–1916), whose powers she believed helped the sickly Alexis, seriously damaged the royal family's reputation.

Devoted to each other and to autocracy: Tsar Nicholas II and Tsaritsa Alexandra. They were married in 1894.

Industrialization

Although deeply conservative, Nicholas was prepared to accept change in one sphere. He understood that Russia needed to industrialize to maintain its position as a great power. Nicholas Bunge, his father's minister of finance (1881–1886), had started the process. Under Sergei Witte (finance minister 1892–1903), the state played a more active role in the industrialization process—with dramatic results.

In the 1890s, Russia's output of coal, iron ore, and petroleum rose between 250 and 350 percent, while the rail network almost doubled in size. By 1900, Russia had risen to fourth among the world's leading industrial producers. The average annual growth rate between 1885 and 1914 was a remarkable 5.7 percent.

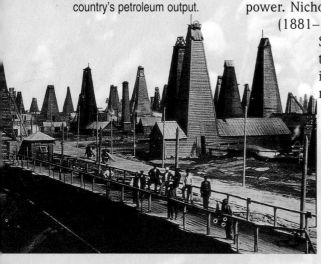

Baku oil wells in the early 20th century. By 1913, the region accounted for four-fifths of the country's petroleum output.

The 1905 Revolution

Following Russia's defeat in the Crimean War (1854–1856), Nicholas' grandfather, Alexander II (ruled 1855–1881), had introduced a number of reforms, including emancipation of the serfs, legal reforms, and a system of elected local councils or *zemstva*. The assassination of the "Tsar Liberator" by a terrorist bomb confirmed both Alexander III's (ruled 1881–1894) and Nicholas II's belief that further reform would be a sign of weakness.

A second military humiliation, this time in the Russo–Japanese War (1904–1905), produced widespread and violent displays of discontent. The mutinies, strikes, and uprisings of the 1905 Revolution forced Nicholas to issue an October Manifesto that granted Russia a form of constitution and consequently divided the opposition. The centerpiece of the new arrangement was an elected central assembly, the Duma. Confronted by liberal and socialist opposition in the first two Dumas (1906 and 1907), Nicholas altered the franchise to ensure that their successors were more supportive of his government. Since the tsar was still technically an autocrat, solely responsible for appointing and dismissing his Council of Ministers, the 1905 Revolution left Russia's system of government much as before—outdated, unresponsive, and widely unpopular.

Fires burning over Moscow during the 1905 Revolution. Fighting lasted in the city until January 1906.

An Unpopular Regime

A wide range of opposition groups had been campaigning for the end of tsarism since at least the 1870s. The first and most obvious reason for this widespread opposition was the tsar's incompetence and inability to compromise. The second was the emergence by the early 20th century of a radically inclined intelligentsia. Men who were well-educated and familiar with the ideas of Western political thinkers, from the liberal John Stuart Mill to the communist Karl Marx, provided the opposition with an intellectual foundation and leadership. Third, the economic and social conditions of the great majority of the tsar's subjects inevitably bred discontent. After the 1905 Revolution, Prime Minister Peter Stolypin (1862–1911) sought to divert rural dissatisfaction by implementing agricultural reforms designed to create a class of wealthy, land-owning peasants. While this met with some success, it did not lessen the dire (and probably increasing) poverty of the majority.

The liberal conservative Peter Stolypin. His assassination by a Socialist Revolutionary Party (SR) terrorist in 1911 deprived the tsar of arguably his most able minister.

By 1914, there were more than 3 million people permanently employed in industry, with perhaps another 4 million peasants migrating to the towns for seasonal work. Close links with the peasantry, ghastly living conditions, long hours, and lamentably poor pay made the urban working class a fertile breeding ground for radical agitation.

Populists and Liberals

Populism, a diverse movement calling for the overthrow of autocracy and redistribution of land, was the principal opposition movement of the 1870s. It was severely repressed following the assassination of Alexander II in 1881. Organized liberal opposition emerged only in the early 20th century. Rejecting violent revolution, it called for a gradual and peaceful transition to a Western-style democracy, with civil rights and the rule of law. By 1917, its principal organization was the Constitutional Democratic Party (Kadet), led by Paul Miliukov (1849–1943).

The Revolutionaries

Initially there were two broadly-based socialist opposition groups, the Socialist Revolutionaries (SRs) and the Social Democrats (SDs). The loosely organized SRs, whose slogan was "Land and Liberty," were hostile to all "exploiting" classes and wanted a democratic republic. They had wide support among peasants and industrial workers.

The Marxist SDs, who included G. V. Plekhanov (1857–1918) and V. I. Lenin (1870–1924) in their ranks, called for a revolution led by the proletariat. Lenin, in his highly influential pamphlet *What Is To Be Done?* (1902), added that this revolution should be organized and led by a small band of professional revolutionaries:

> *...no revolutionary movement can be durable without a stable organization of leaders which preserves continuity.*

Partly because of theoretical and tactical disagreements, and partly because of Lenin's overbearing style of leadership, in 1903 the SDs split between the Bolsheviks (meaning "the majority"), led by Lenin, and the more broadly based and genuinely democratic Mensheviks (meaning "the minority") of Y. O. Martov (1873–1923).

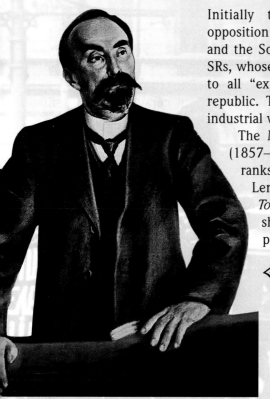

G. V. Plekhanov, who played a key role in converting the radical Russian intelligentsia to Marxism. He died shortly after the Bolshevik seizure of power.

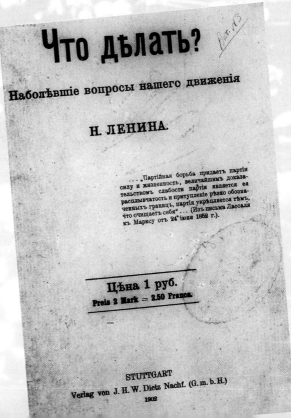

Что дѣлать?

Наболѣвшіе вопросы нашего движенія

Н. ЛЕНИНА.

".... Партійная борьба придаетъ партіи силу и жизненность, величайшимъ доказательствомъ слабости партіи является ея расплывчатость и притупленіе рѣзко обозначенныхъ границъ, партія укрѣпляется тѣмъ, что очищаетъ себя" ... (Изъ письма Лассаля къ Марксу отъ 24 іюня 1852 г.).

Цѣна 1 руб.
Preis 2 Mark = 2.50 Francs.

STUTTGART
Verlag von J. H. W. Dietz Nachf. (G. m. b. H.)
1902

The title page of Lenin's pamphlet *What Is To Be Done?* that introduced into Marxism the concept of a professional revolutionary elite.

Government by Default

The unacceptable face of tsarism: victims of the Lena Goldfields shootings, 1912.

In 1914, the countryside was relatively quiet. The revolutionary movements remained bitterly divided and many of their leaders were in either prison or exile. The army and police were loyal. Liberals had been frustrated by the narrowing of the Duma's power. Industrial production was rising fast, imports were steady, and exports and revenue were at record highs.

All was not well, however. Government ministers, led by puppet premiers after Stolypin's assassination in 1911, failed to show either competence or imagination. In the first half of 1914, 1.3 million industrial workers went on strike. Unjustifiably harsh repressive policies (typified by the shooting of 200 unarmed strikers at the Lena Goldfields in 1912) increased the alienation of Nicholas' out-of-touch regime. However, lack of consensus over how to change the system or what should replace it meant that, for want of something better, tsarism remained.

War

Nicholas II, the "little father" of his people, blesses troops before they leave for the front.

The outbreak of war in August 1914 ushered in two and a half years of anguish and humiliation. As in 1904–1905, military failure magnified the government's mismanagement and fed popular discontent. Defeats by the Germans in 1914 revealed the army's shortage of weapons, particularly machine guns and shells, and highlighted the shortcomings of the commanders and their staff.

In 1915 it was reported that Russian troops stood unarmed in their trenches, waiting to collect rifles from fallen colleagues. General Polivanov told the Council of Ministers in July:

The soldiers are ... exhausted by the continued defeats and retreats. Their confidence in final victory and in their leadership are undermined.

In such circumstances, Nicholas' unilateral decision in August 1915 to take personal command of the army was extremely unwise. Although the military situation improved slightly in 1916, the losses continued to mount, reaching some 5.7 million men by 1917.

The Home Front Crumbles

The outburst of patriotism that had greeted the outbreak of war quickly melted away. Non-governmental organizations, such as the All-Russia Union of Towns, the All-Russia Union of Zemstva, and the War Industries Committee, which had been established spontaneously to help with the war effort, were shocked and frustrated by the government's incompetence. Disillusioned by defeat and mismanagement, in 1915 the Progressive Bloc (a coalition of Duma moderates) asked the tsar to form a National Government. His refusal cost him the support of most educated opinion.

Poor communication and planning brought severe economic disruption. In 1916, the railway system all but collapsed. Petrograd (St Petersburg's new, Russian-sounding name) and Moscow ran short of food and basic necessities such as clothing and fuel. Shortages forced prices up 300 percent, while average wages only doubled. The situation was made worse by refugees streaming east from the battle zones and peasants hoarding grain. By the end of 1916, strikes and riots, often led by desperate women, were commonplace.

Some of the 137,000 Russians captured during the Battle of Tannenberg (August 23–31, 1914), which halted the Russian advance into Germany.

THE REVOLUTION BEGINS

The Situation in January 1917

By the start of 1917, Tsar Nicholas had lost the backing of virtually every section of society. His natural supporters, the nobility and the higher military commanders, had been driven to distraction by his incompetent appointments, his refusal to accept change, and his obvious lack of skill. The middle classes were similarly infuriated by bureaucratic incompetence and the scale of the slaughter at the front.

The catastrophic military losses had fallen hardest on the peasants, whose loyalty was thereby undermined. Moreover, although peasant farmers had benefited from rising grain prices, these gains were offset by the collapse of the transportation system. The alienation of the urban working class has already been noted (page 14). Even more worrisome for the tsar (had he noticed it) was the mounting discontent among soldiers. The old, loyal army of 1914 had been largely wiped out. Replacements mutinied, deserted, and mutilated themselves in increasing numbers. Among all sectors of the working-class, the cry "Down with the war!" became common.

It seems surprising that the tsarist regime endured as long as it did. The reason it lasted into 1917 was the reluctance of any group with leadership potential to make the first move. The upper and middle classes were unwilling to do anything that might hamper military

Enough is enough—Russian peasant recruits deserting the front line in the winter of 1916.

Is this the way Russians should live? A reconstruction of a wounded peasant soldier returning to his desolate family home.

success. Revolutionaries were prevented from taking immediate advantage of the crisis because of internal disagreements and the exile of their leaders.

The pre-war revolutionary groups were deeply divided over matters of principle and tactics. The war added two further bones of contention. First, it opened a rift between "defensists" and "defeatists" (or "internationalists"). Defensists, including many SRs, put defeat of the enemy before revolution, and therefore supported the war effort. Defeatists, including Lenin and the majority of his Bolsheviks, condemned the war as a capitalist–imperialist struggle fought with proletarian blood. In the *April Theses* of 1917, Lenin said,

 In our attitude toward the war not the slightest concession must be made to "revolutionary defensism" … the war on Russia's part unquestionably remains a predatory imperialist war.…

Significantly, by 1917 Lenin's anti-war sentiments (though perhaps not his reasoning) mirrored those of a growing number of Russians.

The second issue dividing the revolutionaries was the extent to which they should cooperate with other anti-government groups. Lenin, typically, wanted his Bolsheviks to act alone. Some Mensheviks and SRs, notably Alexander Kerensky (1881–1970), a socialist Duma deputy and a member of the SR's Trudovik branch, were more pragmatic. They believed cooperating with the Kadets and other opposition parties would eventually benefit the socialist cause. Only time would prove whether they were right.

The People Rise

As far as we know, the outbreak of the Russian Revolution was not planned; it simply emerged out of chaos and suffering. On January 9, 1917, the Workers Group of the War Industries Committee chose to mark the anniversary of Bloody Sunday (a massacre that had ignited the 1905 Revolution) with a massive strike in the capital. Forty percent of Petrograd's industrial workforce took part. The minister of the Interior, Alexander Protopopov (1866–1918), ordered the arrest of the leaders and stationed Cossack troops in the city.

Another major strike took place on February 14, after which strikes and demonstrations became daily events. On February 22, when workers' leaders held talks with the Duma socialist leader Kerensky, the unrest took on a political dimension. The following day, International Women's Day, female textile workers began a wave of unrest that eventually involved one-third of the Petrograd workforce. The police broke up some demonstrations, but army units called in to restore order showed reluctance to use force.

The eve of the Revolution: workers from Petrograd's many textile factories mark International Women's Day with a massive anti-government demonstration, February 23, 1917.

Nicholas Intervenes

On February 24, factory activists organized further protests and the number on strike rose to 200,000.

Once again, the police and soldiers (many of whom were new recruits from the Petrograd region) appeared of two minds about how to react. On February 25, there were increased strikes, demonstrations, and violence, including attacks on individual police officers and police stations. Students and middle-class sympathizers swelled the workers' ranks.

The military commander of Petrograd, General Khabalov, believing the protests would gradually lose momentum and die away, had so far used a minimum of force against the demonstrators. However, on February 25, he received the following telegram from the tsar:

 I order you to bring all of these disorders in the Capital to a halt as of tomorrow.

At last, Nicholas was going to influence events directly —but not in the manner he imagined.

Mutiny

Khabalov did as he was ordered. Workers flooding into the downtown on Sunday, February 26, found their way blocked by ranks of armed soldiers. When the demonstrators refused to disperse, the soldiers opened fire. Some shots passed over the crowd's heads, but others struck home. By nightfall, several hundred demonstrators had been killed.

The violence had a shattering effect on those ordered to carry it out. During the night of February 26–27, the non-commissioned officers of the Volynsky Guard Regiment, which had been in the forefront of the shootings, took stock of their position and decided not to participate in further repression. In the morning they shot their commanding officer and sent messengers to other military detachments, urging them to join the mutiny, which they gladly did. By the end of the day, the government's authority in the capital had collapsed.

Soldiers patrolling the streets of Petrograd in early February 1917. Pivotol to the February Revolution's success was the unwillingness of such men to act against their fellow citizens.

A government in waiting? A meeting of the state Duma in Petrograd, 1917.

The Duma...

On February 27, demonstrators had the run of the capital. They released political prisoners and sacked the Ministry of the Interior and the headquarters of the secret police. They even occupied the Winter Palace, the tsar's Petrograd residence. Their looting and destruction focused on destroying symbols of tsardom: portraits, images, emblems, and flags.

Nicholas rejected his ministers' request for a Duma-led administration and announced he would return to his capital. Although the Revolution was leaderless, he was hardly the man to fill the vacuum. The obvious source of a new government was the Duma. On February 27, reform-minded Duma members defied the tsar's order suspending their assembly and formed a temporary committee to restore law and order to the capital.

A meeting of the Petrograd Soviet in 1917. The Soviet's famous "Order No. 1" sought to wrest control of the armed forces from the hands of the Duma.

...and the Soviet

Simultaneously, however, socialist leaders (mostly Mensheviks) met to form a Soviet (Council) of Workers' and Soldiers' Deputies, made up of elected workers, intellectuals, and, most importantly, soldiers. This meant Petrograd now had two temporary governments. Significantly, it was the Soviet, through its soldier-instigated "Order No. 1," that took control of the military:

The orders of the military commission of the State Duma shall be executed only in such cases as they do not conflict with the orders and resolutions of the Soviet of Workers' and Soldiers' Deputies.

Provisional Government

By March 3, the Duma Committee and the Soviet Executive Committee had agreed to a new Provisional Government, headed by Prince Lvov (1861–1925). It was dominated by the Kadet party. The Soviet tolerated the new government, but all its members except one refused to join what they believed was a "bourgeois" institution. The exception was Kerensky who, as a consequence, put himself in a position of enormous influence and power.

By now, news of the Revolution had been telegraphed around the empire. It was met with almost universal approval. Crowds demonstrated their delight and hastily formed public committees that were mostly dominated by the middle classes, who quickly took over the authority of imperial officials. As in Petrograd, workers' soviets also sprang up, sometimes including soldiers' deputies.

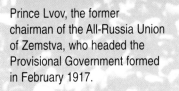

Prince Lvov, the former chairman of the All-Russia Union of Zemstva, who headed the Provisional Government formed in February 1917.

"Look on my works, ye Mighty, and despair!" Children inspect the head of a massive statue of Alexander III that had been toppled during the Revolution.

Republic

Only one act remained, to conclude the first stage of the Revolution (traditionally known as the February Revolution). On February 27 Tsar Nicholas, as out of touch as ever, had talked of using regular troops to crush the rebellion. His orders were countermanded by senior officers, who were on good terms with moderate reformers in the Duma.

Amid the chaos, Nicholas attempted to return home by train. On March 2, he was stranded at Pskov, some 300 miles (480 km) south of Petrograd. Here his senior commanders told him to abdicate. He agreed, passing on his title to his brother, Grand Prince Michael. The following day, the Grand Prince met with leaders of the Provisional Government. When they told him that they could not guarantee his safety, he declined the crown. Russia was now a republic.

Hopes and Aspirations

The principal significance of the tsar's abdication was symbolic. It deprived the Russian Empire of its one focal point, leaving a broad variety of nationalities and economic and social groupings. They were united by a common inheritance, the most pressing aspect of which was the war, but little else.

The peasants hoped to complete the process begun in 1861: returning all land to its "rightful" owners and re-establishing the village community at the heart of society. The industrial working class expected an immediate improvement in their lives—better pay and conditions, and a shorter working day. A good number also anticipated political changes of a democratic socialist nature.

The Bourgeoisie and the Army

It is difficult to make any generalization about the middle classes. However, in March 1917, it seems that most thought that Russia would swiftly join the community of Western liberal democracies. Freed from bureaucratic autocracy, they saw Russia playing a positive role in defeating the German–Austrian enemy.

This view, essentially the program of the Kadets, was hardly shared by the common soldiers. Most of them—ill-trained peasants stuffed into military uniform—

The disillusion is total: Russian soldiers bearing republican banners, 1917.

wanted the war to end so they could go home. At worst, they wanted the continuation of a defensive war with no more costly offensives. The American journalist John Reed, in his *Ten Days That Shook the World*, remembered one soldier addressing a crowd:

 Comrades, the people at the top are always calling upon us to sacrifice more, sacrifice more, while those who have everything are left unmolested.

New Hopes for the Nationalities

To the non-Russian "nationalities," the overthrow of the tsar raised hopes of an end to the hated process of Russification. The more radical nationalist groups, such as the Ukrainian Central Rada (Council), wanted full independence within a Russian federation. Finnish nationalists went further, claiming that links between themselves and Russia were now severed.

Left to right: Irakli Tsereteli, the SR leader who joined the Provisional Government in May 1917 and served for a while as Minister of the Interior; Nikolai Chkheidze, a Menshevik Duma deputy; Fedor Dan, a Menshevik leader.

Revolutionaries Divided

Revolutionaries of all persuasions were agreed upon one thing: The events of February–March 1917 marked only the beginning of the Russian Revolution. There was little agreement, however, about how it should continue. As before, two issues marked a major fault line: cooperation with the liberals and the war.

The moderate left position was typified by the stance of Irakli Tsereteli, a Menshevik who returned from Siberian exile in March 1917. He sought a defensive war ("revolutionary defensism") leading to a negotiated peace, an elected democracy, and limited support for the Provisional Government until Russia was ready to move from its bourgeois phase to become truly socialist.

The radical left position was typified by Lenin. He was its outstanding figure, although his influence was limited until April 1917, when he returned from exile in Switzerland. Believing Russia was ripe for a genuinely socialist revolution, he condemned revolutionary defensism and the Provisional Government outright, and called for Russia immediately to quit the "imperialist–capitalist" war.

THE PROVISIONAL GOVERNMENT

The Problems of the Provisional Government

With such diverse popular expectations, the Provisional Government could not hope to please everyone. As it was, it managed to satisfy the wishes of very few and collapsed as it had begun—in revolution—after holding power for only seven and a half months.

The Kadet-dominated first Provisional Government (there were several changes of ministry) did not represent the people at large. Its leader, Prince Lvov, was a liberal aristocrat, its foreign minister, Paul Miliukov (1849–1943), a Kadet, and its war minister, Alexander Guchkov (1862–1936), a Duma conservative.

The ministry was hampered by its liberal scruples. The removal of censorship and granting of the freedom of the press and of assembly helped its opponents. Moreover, since it was "provisional" it believed it had the moral authority to keep things ticking only until the meeting of an elected constituent assembly. By the time this assembly finally gathered (1918), the Provisional Government was no more. Meanwhile, interim measures to maintain law and order, such as establishing local *zemstvo* chairmen as law officers (commissars), were generally resented.

The government felt bound to honor treaty obligations to foreign powers and ignored popular demands for peace. Indeed, some of its members believed war was a useful cover for taking a strong line against the revolutionaries. John Reed recalled bourgeois diners saying they would rather be ruled by Germans than by Bolsheviks.

The leaders of the first Provisional Government. Communists regarded the unelected, Kadet-dominated ministry with deep suspicion.

Alexander Kerensky, the only socialist member of the first Provisional Government, photographed in 1917. He fled abroad after the Bolshevik Revolution and spent the rest of his life in France, Australia, and, from 1946 on, the U.S.

The Soviet Threat

The network of socialist soviets, especially the highly influential Petrograd Soviet, further weakened the Provisional Government. Relations were inevitably strained between a government intent on stopping revolution, and socialists, enjoying strong popular support, who believed further revolution was inevitable. A major confrontation started on March 14, when the Petrograd Soviet issued an international "appeal" to fellow socialists for the "monstrous war" to end:

 ...we announce that the time has come to start a decisive struggle against the grasping ambitions of the governments of all countries.

New Government, Old Policies

The Soviet, headed by Tsereteli after March 22 and backed by an All-Russia Conference of Soviets of Workers' and Soldiers' Deputies, forced the government to send a message to its allies denouncing territorial annexations. When Miliukov attached a conciliatory covering letter, there were widespread protests. The outcome was a new coalition Provisional Government (May 5) from which Miliukov was excluded and in which Kerensky was joined by five more socialists, including Tsereteli.

Believing, illogically, that it would hasten peace, Socialist Revolutionary defensists supported a military offensive launched on June 18. Its collapse, with huge casualties, by July 5 alienated the unelected government still further. Moreover, by discrediting revolutionary defensism it also played into the hands of Lenin, who had stuck firmly to his criticism of the war set out in his *April Theses* (April 4, 1917).

Paul Miliukov, the Kadet foreign minister of the first Provisional Government. He was committed to Russia's remaining at war with Germany.

The Failure of the Provisional Government

By July 1917, the Provisional Government was deeply unpopular. It had failed to meet the demands of the Bolshevik slogan, "Peace, Bread, Land!" Its non-socialist majority still wanted military victory. There were food shortages in the major cities, despite a government grain monopoly, price-fixing, and some ineffective rationing. The peasants, infuriated by the lack of land redistribution, had started to seize the property of the nobility and wealthier landowners.

Although industrial workers had been granted an eight-hour working day (March–April), by the summer industrial breakdown was driving them into militant action. The Ukraine was granted limited self-government on July 1 (causing the resignation of Kadet ministers) and four days later, Finland proclaimed itself self-governing.

This mounting chaos did not benefit the Soviet's revolutionary defensist majority. The socialists in the Provisional Government were identified with the failed June–July offensive. Furthermore, ministerial authority involved them in painful decisions. On July 17, for example, Tsereteli, now minister of the Interior, ordered action against peasants who unlawfully seized land not belonging to them. The decision was unenforceable, and the countryside continued to slip from the government's control.

Anti-government street protests in Petrograd during the July Days, 1917. The demonstrations led to the arrest of several prominent Bolsheviks.

July Days

The next great crisis was the "July Days," a massive anti-government protest by troops, sailors, and workers in Petrograd on July 3–5. When the SRs, Mensheviks, and Bolsheviks failed to provide leadership and organization (Lenin arrived late from Finland), the demonstrations petered out. The Provisional Government, reformed with Kerensky as minister-president, staggered on. Radicals criticized the Bolsheviks for failing to lead the uprising, and the government blamed them (falsely) for organizing it. Several Bolshevik leaders, including L. D. Trotsky (1879–1940), who had recently come over from the Mensheviks, were arrested. Lenin returned to Finland for his own safety.

The Kornilov Affair

The Bolshevik position was restored by a confused episode known as the "Kornilov affair" of August 27–31, 1917. A growing number of liberal and right-wing politicians believed that only military dictatorship could save Russia from the militant left. A. M. Maslennikov, in a private session of the State Duma on July 18, had described the militant left as:

Those dreamers and lunatics who imagine they are creators of world politics....

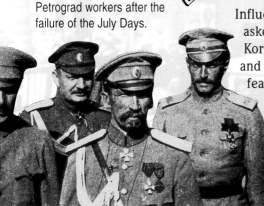

General Kornilov (center) and his staff in August 1917. The general's unsuccessful coup enabled the Bolsheviks to regain the support of the Petrograd workers after the failure of the July Days.

Influenced by such opinions, it seems that Kerensky asked the new supreme army commander, General Kornilov, to occupy the capital with reliable troops and suppress a supposed Bolshevik coup. Then, fearing that Kornilov would turn against him, Kerensky changed sides. He rallied the Soviet to Petrograd's defense, ordered the release of imprisoned Bolshevik leaders, and called on the Red Guards (armed factory workers, increasingly pro-Bolshevik) to thwart the coup. While infiltrators undermined the morale of Kornilov's forces, railway workers slowed their advance. The coup collapsed on August 31, and Kornilov was arrested the following day. In the aftermath, Kerensky's credibility plummeted, army discipline crumbled, and the popularity of the radical left, particularly the Bolsheviks, soared.

Red troops arriving in Petrograd, August 1917, to put down Kornilov's coup.

Leon Trotsky joined the Bolsheviks in the summer of 1917 and played a leading role in the October Revolution. He was expelled from the USSR in 1929 and murdered by Soviet agents in Mexico in 1940.

The Bolshevik Takeover

By September 9, the Bolsheviks had a majority in the Petrograd Soviet. Two weeks later, Trotsky became its chairman. Lenin, the Provisional Government's most feared opponent, remained in exile.

Despite the Bolsheviks' mounting popularity (between February and October, membership grew from 10,000 to 300,000), their Central Committee was reluctant to plan an armed uprising. However, Lenin returned to Petrograd on October 10. He believed history would not forgive them if they failed to organize a revolution immediately, and he persuaded a majority of his colleagues to change their minds. The Bolshevik-dominated Soviet organized a Military Revolutionary Committee (MRC), supposedly to defend the capital from the Germans but really to prepare for revolution. By October 22, the party was instigating pro-Soviet rallies and infiltrating the Petrograd garrison.

Russia was now in a state of total collapse. Strikes, lock-outs, demonstrations, and occupations were part of everyday urban life. Crime was rising, while food supplies and industrial output were falling. With "revolution" on everyone's lips, people were certain something dramatic was going to happen.

The Bolsheviks were assisted by two strokes of good fortune. First, a second meeting of the Congress of Soviets, representing city and provincial soviets across Russia, was postponed from October 20 to October 25. Second, on October 24 Kerensky ordered the seizure of Bolshevik printing presses. This forced the Bolsheviks to act, before the Congress (where the Bolsheviks were outnumbered 300 delegates to 660) could intervene.

A detachment of Red Guards on the streets of Petrograd, October 1917.

On October 24, Trotsky organized the seizure of the telephone exchange, railway stations, and the central Post Office. The Red Guards met with little resistance, and by nightfall most of the city's key points were in revolutionary hands. Lenin emerged from hiding at 2 A.M. on October 25, determined to present the Congress with a *fait accompli*. Taking control of the Bolshevik headquarters in the Smolny Institute, he launched an all-out Bolshevik offensive. First, on October 25, the MRC (carefully avoiding the word "Bolshevik") declared that the Provisional Government was deposed. It explained,

The State Power has passed into the hands of the … Military Revolutionary Committee, which stands at the head of the Petrograd proletariat and garrison.

Kerensky fled. Red Guards occupied the rest of the city, apart from the Winter Palace where the Provisional Government continued to sit in impotent splendor. They were eventually arrested at 2 A.M. on October 26.

The Second Congress of Soviets met at 10:40 P.M. on October 25. The sound of gunfire from the Peter and Paul fortress, shooting (inaccurately) at the Winter Palace, convinced radical SRs and Mensheviks to join with the Bolsheviks in a show of revolutionary unity. The moderates then walked out, leaving Lenin and his Bolsheviks in control of the Congress and the capital.

The storming of the Winter Palace, the headquarters of the Provisional Government, on October 26, 1917 (top), and the damage the next morning (below).

Bolshevik Success

The Bolshevik seizure of power in Petrograd in October 1917 was due only partly to the activities of the revolutionaries. Their preparations and daring were important, of course, but the "October Revolution" was truly a popular revolution, an expression of the people's will. The genius of the Bolshevik leadership lay in recognizing that will and using it to its own ends.

The Bolsheviks entered a power vacuum created by the failure of the Provisional Government. It was discredited in all it did, from the incompetent attempt to introduce food rationing to its disastrous summer offensive and its involvement in the Kornilov coup. It was rife with divisions and unable to keep its most basic promise—to establish a constituent assembly.

The Bolsheviks also benefited from mistakes made by the moderate revolutionaries, particularly their endorsement of revolutionary defensism and participation in the Provisional Government. Moreover, the Bolsheviks alone learned the lesson of the July Days and acted when the situation presented itself.

The Bolsheviks and the People

Far from imposing their platform on the people, as has sometimes been said, the Bolsheviks listened and gave voice to popular aspirations. As John Reed observed,

> *...they took the crude, simple desires of the workers, soldiers, and peasants, and from them built their program. And so, while the ... Mensheviki and the Socialist revolutionaries involved themselves in compromise with the bourgeoisie, the Bolsheviki rapidly captured the Russian masses.*

The slogan "All Power to the Soviets" tapped into the general despair at upper- and middle-class control, both in politics and the workplace. "Peace, Bread, Land!" appealed directly to the disaffected soldiers and their wives, the poverty-stricken urban masses, and the disillusioned peasantry.

The power of propaganda—a Bolshevik supporter hands out tracts to eager supporters. The Bolsheviks' triple demand—"Peace, Bread, Land!"—had immense popular appeal.

The fact that the Bolshevik coup was over in 36 hours and achieved with a minimum of bloodshed supports the view that they rode to power on a wave of near-universal support (or indifference). The ruthlessness with which they then extended their power must not blind us to this.

Luck and Lenin

Luck, of course, had played its part. Kerensky's blunder over the Kornilov affair restored Bolshevik fortunes after the July Days. Other events assisted the Bolsheviks: the decision to postpone the Congress of Soviets to allow all delegates to attend, the attack on the Bolshevik presses, and the shooting that alarmed the radical-left delegates at the initial meeting of the Congress.

Lenin, the inspiration, engine, and principal organizer of the Bolshevik Revolution.

Nevertheless, fortune, as the saying goes, favors the brave. And in Lenin the Bolsheviks had a brave, bold leader whose resolution, determination, tactical ability, and skill as a propagandist were far greater than those of any of his rivals. In the last instance, it was he who made the revolution his own.

Members of Moscow's urban proletariat being recruited into the Red Army, spring 1918.

THE GRIP TIGHTENS

Sovnarkom

On October 26, the Bolsheviks announced a program that promised working-class opponents of the Provisional Government almost everything they had demanded, including peace, land to the peasants, democracy in the army, and worker control of factories. Later, they issued more specific decrees on the questions of peace and land, and established a new (theoretically provisional) government: the Council of People's Commissars (Sovnarkom). Its membership was entirely Bolshevik, headed by Lenin.

The regime's first tasks were to consolidate its position in Petrograd and expand its power base. Between October 27–30, forces loyal to the Bolsheviks thwarted a military counter-coup organized by Kerensky and General Krasnov. A second threat came from excluded SRs and Mensheviks. The SR newspaper *Dyelo Naroda* (People's Cause) declared of the Bolsheviks:

> *They make golden promises to the masses, knowing in advance that they can fulfill none of them …. The Bolsheviks are the most dangerous enemies of the Revolution.*

The SRs failed to act, however, and were diverted by protracted and ultimately fruitless negotiations. Only in December, prior to the meeting of the Constituent Assembly, did Lenin reluctantly bring leftist SRs into the government.

Strikers at a Petrograd factory, 1917. The high concentration of industrial wage earners in the capital made it the obvious focal point for a socialist revolution.

The Spread of Bolshevism

Bolshevik power spread swiftly in areas where the party was strong, principally the industrial north. By November 2, the Bolsheviks were victorious in Moscow (after several days of fierce fighting) and had extended their control into the Volga region. By December, they were in charge of most towns in north and central European Russia. Yet their influence remained minimal in vast areas, including most of the countryside and the regions occupied by non-Russians.

At the front, on receiving news of the Bolshevik coup, several units negotiated unofficial armistices. On December 2, an official month-long armistice with Germany and Austria–Hungary was declared.

Reform...

Following an optimistic-sounding "Declaration of the Rights of the People of Russia," government pronouncements abolished ranks and titles, replaced the law courts with revolutionary tribunals, reformed marriage and divorce, separated church and state, and replaced the old Julian calendar with the Gregorian one. A free and universal education system was promised. Economic decrees cancelled government debts and nationalized the banks. Workplaces remained in private ownership but were placed under worker supervision. A comprehensive system of social security was proposed.

A stylized Soviet painting depicting Lenin (center left) and Stalin (center right) with Felix Dzerzhinsky (right), at the founding of the Bolshevik counterrevolutionary organization, Cheka.

...and Repression

However, other developments reflected the growing authoritarianism of the Bolshevik leadership. Press censorship was imposed on October 27. The Bolsheviks took over the army headquarters on November 20 and a week later arrested the Kadet leadership. Following a damaging strike by government white-collar workers, the party leadership established Cheka, a commission for fighting counter-revolution and sabotage, in December. Headed by Felix Dzerzhinsky (1877–1926), it became a ruthless police force operating against dissidents.

The Constituent Assembly

The Bolsheviks had promised to pursue the Provisional Government's plan for a Constituent Assembly. However, the elections of November 2 were a serious disappointment. Although the Bolsheviks polled 10 million votes (about 24 percent), giving them 168 seats, they were swamped by massive peasant support for the SRs, who obtained 48 percent of the vote and 370 seats out of the total 703.

Lenin and the Bolshevik leadership immediately tried to belittle the Assembly, claiming that soviets were a "higher form of democracy" than a parliamentary assembly. They made it clear that, if necessary, they would dissolve the Assembly by force. Support for the Assembly wavered, too, as peasants and workers were persuaded that their interests were sufficiently represented in the Congress of Soviets and Sovnarkom.

The Brest–Litovsk peace conference, 1918, at which the Bolsheviks agreed to surrender vast tracts of western Russia to Germany.

Brest-Litovsk

It was no surprise, therefore, when the Constituent Assembly was forcibly dissolved on January 6, the day after it met. This high-handed action confirmed the moderates' mistrust of the Bolsheviks, who, they said, were now appearing in their true, authoritarian colors. Events at the front added to the Bolsheviks' difficulties. Trotsky, Sovnarkom's foreign minister, failed to negotiate a lasting peace, and in February the Germans advanced into the Ukraine and the Baltic provinces. The German commander wrote in his diary,

No other way is possible, otherwise the brutes [the Bolsheviks] will ... quietly get together a new revolutionary army and turn the whole of Europe into a pig-sty.

Unable to resist, the Bolsheviks were forced to accept humiliating terms in the Treaties of Brest-Litovsk (February and March 1918). The first treaty recognized the independence of the Ukraine, though it was really under German control. The second, agreed to by the Bolshevik leadership only when Lenin threatened to resign, brought peace at an enormous price. Russia surrendered most of its western territories, including

60 million people (34 percent of the total population), 32 percent of its arable land, 25 percent of its railways, 33 percent of its factories, and 75 percent of its coal and iron ore production.

Civil War

Brest-Litovsk was a desperate humiliation. Twelve days after it was signed, the leftist SRs walked out of the government, and by summer the Bolsheviks (restyled as Communists or Soviets) were surrounded by hostile forces—various groups of "Whites" who were opposed to the "Red" Communists.

Admiral Kolchak (1874–1920) raised a White army in Siberia, General Denikin (1872–1947) another in the south. Germans, nationalists, and Soviets battled for the Ukraine. Finland, Poland, and the Baltic states were already lost, and it seemed Georgia, Armenia, and Azerbaijan might well go the same way. The Communists even faced Allied soldiers, ostensibly sent to Archangel and Murmansk to fight the Germans. So, when in May 1918 30,000 Czech ex-prisoners of war fell out with local Communists and seized a large section of the Trans-Siberian railway, the Communist government found itself fighting a full-scale civil war.

Czech ex-prisoners of war formed a unit to fight against the Reds in the Civil War. They are here photographed on the Trans-Siberian railway.

The Whites...

The Communist regime was born out of war and had been fighting its enemies in one guise or another since the Kerensky–Krasnov attempted countercoup of October 1917. Nevertheless, the threat that had emerged by the summer of 1918 was, on paper at least, overwhelming and obliged Lenin to transfer his capital from Petrograd to the less vulnerable Moscow.

The White forces were made up of a motley collection of tsarists, Kadets, right SRs, Mensheviks, and maverick Cossacks and Czechs. They, together with the nationalist forces (including Finns, Poles, Ukrainians, and Georgians), were supported by detachments from the British Empire, France, Italy, Serbia, and the United States. To complicate matters further, Romanians encroached in the west and Japanese (shadowed by Americans) in the east, while anarchists and "Green Armies" of peasants preyed on Reds and Whites alike.

White soldiers stand over the dead bodies of their enemies. Horrific atrocities were committed by both sides in the Civil War.

...and the Reds

Trotsky, appointed commissar for war (head of the Supreme Military Council) in March 1918, led the Red war effort. The first test for his embryonic Red Army (see page 41) was to counter the threat from the east. During the summer the Kolchak–Czech alliance advanced beyond Ekaterinburg (where the Communists shot the captive tsar and his family) to Samara and Kazan, and established a short-lived "Volga Republic." However, by the end of September, Trotsky's energetic response had halted this advance and brought Kazan back under Red control.

1919

1919 was the key year of the war. The Reds faced three separate offensives. Admiral Kolchak resumed his advance in the east. General Denikin moved up from the south, taking Kharkov, Tsaritsyn (the future Stalingrad), and Kiev. In October he was within 250 miles (400 km) of Moscow.

Playing the nationalist card: a Bolshevik cartoon depicting the White generals Denikin, Kolchak, and Yudenich as dogs controlled by foreign powers (the U.S., France, and Britain).

A detachment of the Red Army, 1920. Based around units of the Red Guards and men from the old tsarist army, by the end of the Civil War it had become a well-organized and effective fighting force.

Meanwhile, in the west, General Yudenich (1862–1933) closed in on Petrograd. All three offensives, planned and fought with little coordination, eventually petered out. The ruthlessness of the well-organized Red resistance is captured by Lenin's chillingly honest comment:

If we are not ready to shoot a saboteur and White Guardist, what sort of revolution is that?

In 1919, Trotsky arrived in Petrograd in time to save the city. The following year Kolchak was betrayed to the Bolsheviks and shot. General Wrangel (1878–1928) replaced the defeated Denikin in the south, failed with a fresh offensive, and saw the remnants of his defeated army evacuated from Sevastopol.

The War Ends

The Poles joined the conflict in April 1919 and moved into the Ukraine. Here they were halted and driven back to the outskirts of Warsaw. A subsequent Polish counter-offensive had cleared the Reds from much of Poland by the time peace was made at Riga in March 1921. Although Japanese forces remained until 1922, Riga marked the end of significant fighting.

After surrendering to the Allies in 1918, Germany and Austria–Hungary had evacuated the possessions ceded to them at Brest-Litovsk. Now, after three years of civil war, the Communists had brought the bulk of this territory under the control of Moscow.

Red Victory

Part of the explanation for Red success in the Civil War lay in the weaknesses and failings of the Whites. Kolchak, Denikin, and Yudenich, all able and experienced commanders, fought separate campaigns with no central command or supply structure. Their remote territorial bases were weak, and the regional governments they established (such as the Volga Republic) lacked reliable bureaucracies and local administrations, and were not served by the main communication networks running along the Petrograd–Moscow axis.

The diverse nature of the White forces—tsarists, Kadets, right SRs, Mensheviks, and others—was another problem. Although they clearly knew what they did not want (communism), their disagreement over what should replace Lenin's regime deprived them of a unifying goal. Moreover, two proposed alternatives—tsarism and the Provisional Government—were deeply discredited.

Two Communist propaganda posters of 1920. The top one declares 'The White Poles will never lord it over the workers" while the other cries "Wrangel is still alive!"

Weak Support

The Whites also failed to band together with the nationalist movements. If they had accepted the independence of Finland, Estonia, and Latvia, for example, they could have boosted their standing in the Baltic region. "Independent" forces such as the Green Armies, although hostile to both sides, inclined toward the Reds, whom they saw as more sympathetic to the cause of the common people.

The support of the Western powers was at best halfhearted. Exhausted by four years of devastating war and sensitive to popular cries of "hands off the soviets," after November 1918 their efforts were largely tokenistic. Finally, the Whites always had difficulty in recruiting to the ranks.

The Red Army

In contrast, the Reds fought under Trotsky's unified, energetic, and ruthless command. Their goal was simple and focused: to save the Revolution. The White's association with foreign powers made the Red cause the patriotic one, too. The peasantry, no great friend of the Communists, still tended toward a regime that accepted the land seizures of 1917.

The development of an effective Red Army from 1918 onward was perhaps the major reason for the Communist victory. It was created from scratch around the Red Guards and pro-Bolshevik units of the old army and navy. By 1921, it numbered 5 million. However, only 10 percent were fighting troops—the bulk of peasant recruits worked in the support services.

A Communist poster celebrating victory in the Civil War and exhorting the nation to work. The caption reads, "We have defeated the enemy with our arms, now we shall get bread by hard work."

Ideology and Terror

Because winning the Civil War was a matter of life or death (literally) for the Communist leadership, they turned the army into the country's principal bureaucracy. A system which Lenin later called "War Communism" (see page 43) geared production and distribution to the war effort. Ideological niceties, such as the election of officers, were replaced by traditional discipline and appointment on merit. Some 50,000 ex-tsarist officers were employed (usually shadowed by Communist commissars). Cheka expanded with a hundred-fold increase in employees into a ruthless secret police force dedicated to eliminating all the communists' perceived opponents. Dzerzhinsky made no bones about his brutal methods:

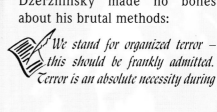

We stand for organized terror – this should be frankly admitted. Terror is an absolute necessity during

ESTABLISHING GOVERNMENT

The Rise of the Party

Before 1917, the Communist leaders had directed all their energies toward seizing power. Furthermore, they believed their revolution would be simply the beginning of a worldwide proletarian revolution after which individual states would cease to matter. When this failed to happen, they were forced to apply themselves to the more ordinary matter of running their country.

A unified government was hindered by the division of political power between Sovnarkom, the Central Executive Committee of Soviets, and the Communist Party (especially its Political Bureau or "Politburo"). A hierarchy of authority emerged during the Civil War, with the Party gaining supremacy over the soviets, and the Politburo developing into the central organ of totalitarian, one-party rule.

Communism equals feminism? A propaganda poster showing a woman reaching from a life of drudgery toward the goal of communism.

Social Change

As all citizens ("comrades") were theoretically equal, the Communists' opponents predicted swift social collapse. This did not happen. Women were the largest group to benefit, helped by full legal rights (although of limited worth in a totalitarian state), marriage as an equal and dissolvable partnership, the legalization of abortion, and special women's departments within the Party. Even so, few women rose to positions of power and it was years before legal change had an impact on provincial and rural life.

A handful of radical thinkers condemned the family as a "bourgeois" institution. One Civil War slogan apparently read,

Down with the capitalist tyranny of parents!

The adoption of "free love" in some circles inevitably attracted attention. However, this interpretation of the Marxist idea of holding all things in common—including love—was not widely followed, nor was it approved of by the morally conventional Lenin.

War Communism

The most dramatic changes were economic. Marxism condemned the free market and private property, and believed wealth should be shared according to need. These were the principles behind War Communism. Historians disagree as to whether the policy was introduced for theoretical or practical reasons, but the fact that it was relaxed once the war was over suggests the latter.

The rapid nationalization of large industrial concerns began in 1918. A similar policy for smaller enterprises was launched in 1920 and proceeded more slowly. The Provisional Government's grain monopoly and rationing had limited the free market before the Communist takeover. After 1917, it disappeared altogether. Inflation skyrocketed (1922 prices were over seven-*million* times those of 1913), money lost all meaning, and barter became the common means of exchange. By 1920, even wages were being paid in kind.

In rural areas, changes occurred only slowly. The Party's problem was one of perception: Their communism meant large-scale enterprise under public ownership, while peasant communism meant a restoration of the traditional, small-scale *mir* community. Faced with widespread peasant resistance under the embarrassing slogan "Down with the Communists! Long Live the Bolsheviks!," the Party trod carefully. It seized grain where it could, set up a few collective farms, and tried to inspire a class war between rich and poor peasants.

The misery of the Civil War: A Russian family receives aid at a famine relief center, 1921. Famine and disease caused greater loss of life than military action during the Civil War.

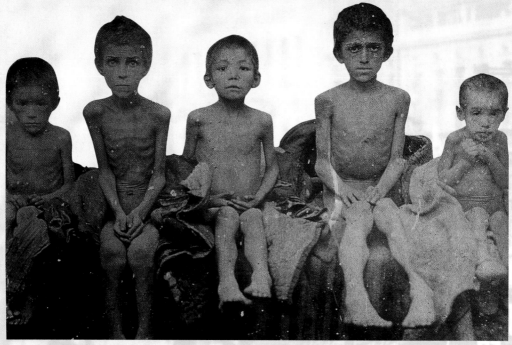

Child famine victims, 1921. In some parts of the country, peasants resorted to cannibalism to stay alive during the Civil War.

The Condition of Russia

By 1921, the Communist state (which in 1922 became the Union of Soviet Socialist Republics, or USSR) was in a precarious condition. Between 1917 and 1921, war, famine, and inept economic management had resulted in 10 million deaths (5 million from starvation), crippling inflation, a 40 percent fall in grain production, a collapse in large-scale industrial output to 18 percent of its 1913 level, and urban decline (the population of Petrograd dwindled from 2.5 million in 1917 to 750,000 in 1920).

Nor were popular grievances just economic. The Bolsheviks came to power on a wave of popular enthusiasm for their "Peace, Bread, Land" policy and promises of power to the soviets. Instead of peace, the people had civil war; instead of bread, they had famine; instead of being secure in their farms, they faced a regime wanting state ownership of land; instead of power resting with elected soviets, it was siphoned off into the hands of unelected Party officials and the terrifying Cheka.

Rebellion and Reaction

In February 1921, the sailors of the Kronstadt naval base, who had played a key role in helping the Bolsheviks to power, rose in rebellion. Troops numbering 50,000 were brought in, and the revolt was crushed.

A month later, Lenin announced an official end to free discussion (or "factionalism"):

> *...discussion means disputes; disputes mean discord; discord means that Communists have become weak.*

Cheka (reorganized as the GPU in 1922) was given the job of enforcing tighter political discipline through show trials, executions, and deporting opponents to one of the 315 concentration camps in place by 1923. SRs, Mensheviks, dissenting Bolsheviks, and uncooperative peasants all suffered. The new dictatorship was more ruthless than anything experienced under the tsars.

Fighting during the rebellion at the Kronstadt naval base, 1921. The authorities dismissed the revolt as "a bourgeois-inspired counterrevolutionary insurgence."

A show trial conducted by Cheka, which was reorganized as a permanent political police force, the GPU.

New Economic Policy (NEP)

Another new policy was the NEP. This turnabout was a temporary measure to get the economy back on its feet. Its twin pillars were the return to a money economy and limited capitalism. A new ruble was introduced in 1922, backed by the State Bank. Large-scale industry remained in state hands, although it was revitalized by capitalist-style management and economic incentives for higher production. On the other hand, smaller scale enterprises, including peasant farms, were allowed to operate as private businesses, making profits from surpluses and paying taxes on these to the state. In economic terms, it was a victory for the peasants.

How long that victory would last depended on the Party leadership. By 1922, that leadership was about to change. Lenin, badly wounded in the neck by an SR assassination attempt in 1918, had a series of strokes in 1922–1923 that left him unable to speak. Finally, on January 21, 1924, the father and perhaps betrayer of the Russian Revolution died.

What Was the Russian Revolution?

Disagreement over when the Revolution ended is inseparable from definitions of what it was. If it was the collapse of tsarism and its replacement, after a short period of fake democracy, by a Bolshevik government in Petrograd, then the Revolution was over, at the latest, when the Constituent Assembly was closed on January 6, 1918.

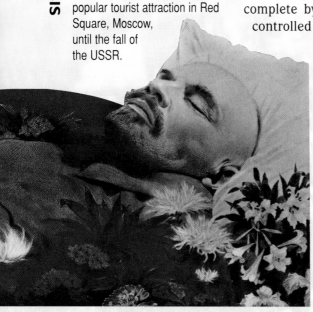

Lenin's preserved body was a popular tourist attraction in Red Square, Moscow, until the fall of the USSR.

To begin with, the Bolshevik takeover was little more than a regional coup. Perhaps the true Revolution was complete by the end of 1921, when the Communists controlled most of the territory of the future USSR. Even then, Cheka/GPU was required to cement one-party rule, and the NEP was needed to restore the battered economy. So perhaps Lenin's death—when production levels were returning to pre-war levels, the countryside was relatively quiet, and the Party was undisputed master of the USSR—is the correct point to declare the Revolution over.

Those who say the Revolution ends later argue that two further changes were needed to meet the aims of the 1917 Bolsheviks: collectivization of agriculture and total state control of all means of production and distribution. These were achieved largely by 1932 (see pages 48–49). Even then, it may be argued that the Revolution was not complete until Stalin had purged all opposition and established himself as undisputed dictator (1938). It is normally agreed, however, that extending the 1917 Revolution into the 1930s broadens its scope too far: Stalin's changes did not so much round off the 1917 Revolution as introduce a "Second Revolution."

The Communist Achievement

What had the Communists achieved by 1924, and how had they done it? In simple political terms, they had established and defended the world's first communist state. In so doing they had come full circle, replacing one authoritarian regime with another.

Social change had been dramatic. The class-ridden Russia of empire, monarchy, nobles, church, landowners, capitalists, workers, and peasants was gone, replaced by a theoretically classless society of equal comrades, male and female. The economic revolution was less complete. Although the state controlled the principal players in the economy, most small businesses and agriculture remained in private (or *mir*) hands. However, the template for future developments was there.

The People's Tragedy

The world's most comprehensive revolution was achieved by a combination of determination, opportunism, and compromise, against a background of divided, short-sighted opposition. The determination, stemming from Lenin, showed itself in acts such as the formation of Cheka and the single-minded pursuit of victory in the Civil War. The coup of October 1917 was the opportunity that paid off, while the NEP illustrated the regime's willingness to compromise. Finally, nothing could have been achieved without the initial support of the Russian masses. It was their tragedy to have been unashamedly betrayed.

"Religion is the opium of the people" (Marx)—soldiers of the Red Army looting a church during the Civil War. The USSR was the world's first officially atheistic regime.

"Lenin sweeps the world clean"—a poster depicting the Soviet leader ridding the world of capitalists, priests, monarchs, and the nobility.

ТОВ. ЛЕНИН ОЧИЩАЕТ ЗЕМЛЮ ОТ НЕЧИСТИ.

CHAPTER SIX

STALINISM

Lenin left a political system dominated by one political party, and a party dominated by one man. Unless democracy were reintroduced (an unrealistic prospect), the system was almost certain to continue into the new era. Trotsky was one candidate for Lenin's role, although he was not an easy man and fellow members of the Politburo were suspicious of his ambition. Other possibilities were G. Zinoviev (1883–1936), head of the Petrograd (now renamed Leningrad) Soviet, and L. Kamenev (1883–1936), head of the Moscow Soviet. In fact, Lenin's successor was neither of these, but a man Lenin himself had warned against:

...he has concentrated enormous power in his hands, and I am not sure that he always knows how to use that power ... [he] is too rude...

This "rude" man was the Communist Party's general secretary, Joseph Dzhugashvili, commonly known as Stalin—"Man of Steel."

Stalin, who dominated the USSR from 1928 to his death in 1953, was the Revolution's darkest legacy. Under his increasingly personal and paranoid rule, the trends evident before 1924—centralization, intolerance, terror, and uneasy relations with other countries—were maintained and magnified.

Centralization was most noticeable in the economic sphere. In 1928, Stalin abandoned the NEP. Gosplan (the state planning office) launched its first Five-Year Plan. Its aim was twofold: first, to boost the USSR's economy (in 1928, for example, steel production was a little less than one-third of that of the United States), and second, to root out remaining private enterprise. This had the additional effect of tightening government control over all citizens.

Industrial output doubled under the first Plan and continued to grow swiftly under the next two (1933–1937, 1938–1942). In the countryside, collective farms replaced individual landholdings. Virtually all cultivated land was farmed collectively by 1938. This

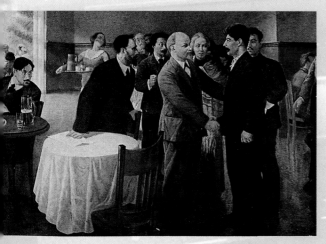

Distorting history: Stalinist propaganda depicts the first meeting between Lenin and Stalin as obviously momentous. Stalin wished to be portrayed as Lenin's heir.

"Farm workers say 'Go.'" A Soviet propaganda image of workers in the Ukraine agreeing to collectivization of agriculture. Imposed for political rather than economic reasons, collectivization gave the government much closer control over peasant communities.

change was fiercely resisted by peasants, who burned crops and slaughtered livestock rather than hand them over to the collective. Collectivization led to the murder of some 5 million peasants. An estimated 10 to 15 million died in the famine of 1932–1934. Millions more simply "disappeared." Agricultural production fell, although it recovered in the mid-1930s.

Intolerance manifested itself in rigid censorship of all the media and arts. The GPU (renamed OGPU in 1924 and NKVD in 1934) maintained ruthless terror against the church, the "bourgeoisie," kulaks (wealthy peasants), and alleged dissidents within the Party. The campaign against the latter came to a head in a series of purges between 1935 and 1938, in which an estimated one million victims were executed (including Zinoviev and Kamenev) and a further 12 million allowed to perish in prison camps.

"Smash the kulaks!" The kulaks, the backbone of Russia's rural economy since Stolypin's time, were ruthlessly weeded out under Stalin's program of collectivization.

The Fascist Threat

Stalin's "Socialism in one country" policy rejected Trotsky's more international approach to communist development, in favor of the USSR going it alone. However, Stalin's USSR could not exist in total isolation from the rest of the world. Soviet Russia emerged from isolation with the 1922 Rapallo Treaty with Germany, which recognized the USSR and got the right to test its weapons secretly in Russia. By 1925 several other powers, including Britain, France, and China (but not the United States), had formally recognized the USSR. Although Stalin still warned of the inevitability of a communist–capitalist clash, he made no attempt to begin such a struggle. Indeed, his "Socialism in one country" policy suggested that it would be postponed indefinitely.

In the 1930s, two developments made Stalin reconsider his independent position: the emergence of Japan as an aggressive militaristic power in the east, and the rise of fascism, particularly in Germany, in the west. The USSR joined the League of Nations in 1934 (a year after Germany and Japan had left), and signed agreements with the Baltic states, Czechoslovakia, Poland, and France. Stalin also sent aid to China to resist Japanese aggression and called on Comintern (the Communist International, formed in 1919 to coordinate communist parties worldwide) to establish an anti-fascist alliance. Germany, Japan, and Italy responded with an Anti-Comintern Pact.

The height of practical arrangements: the signing of the Nazi–Soviet Non-Aggression Pact in August 1939.

Red Army forces defending Stalingrad, 1942. The battle proved to be the turning point in the most brutal war ever fought.

The Great Patriotic War

By 1939, Hitler seemed intent on expanding his Third Reich both west and east toward the USSR. Stalin had lost faith in Great Britain and France's willingness to resist Germany by force and on August 23, 1939, the USSR and Nazi Germany, communist and fascist, signed a Non-Aggression Pact. This possibly cynical act bought Stalin time in which to prepare for war.

On June 22, 1941, Hitler broke the Non-Aggression Pact and launched Operation Barbarossa, a massive invasion of the Soviet Union. The consequent Great Patriotic War was the most costly conflict in human history. Suffering almost unbelievable losses, the Soviets halted the attack on Moscow (1941) and Stalingrad (1942), and in 1943 began to drive back the invader. When Germany finally surrendered in May 1945, the Red Army had freed all Soviet territory and occupied large areas of Eastern Europe, including Poland, Czechoslovakia, Hungary, and eastern Germany.

Superpower

As one eyewitness testified, the war brought massive destruction to the USSR:

> *For thousands of miles, there was not a standing or living object to be seen. Every town was flat.*

Remarkably, two Five-Year Plans (1946–1950 and 1950–1955) swiftly made good the losses and raised industrial and agricultural production well beyond the levels of 1940. Furthermore, the war had left the USSR more or less in control of a vast empire in Eastern Europe. By the time of Stalin's death, the communist Soviet Union and the capitalist United States—locked in a Cold War of nuclear confrontation, misunderstanding, suspicion, and fear—were the world's only superpowers. It was all a far cry from the wishes, even the dreams, of the revolutionaries who had taken to the streets of Petrograd 54 years earlier.

The Red Army enters Budapest, Hungary, 1945. The occupied countries of Eastern Europe remained within the Soviet sphere of influence until 1989.

The Tool of History?

Not surprisingly, since 1953 and particularly since 1991, Stalin's reputation has declined dramatically. An important question about his dictatorship is whether he directed the USSR along paths preordained by the Revolution or whether he abandoned the Revolution and directed the country in a new, Stalinist direction. Some Marxist historians, certainly before the 1990s, tended to the former point of view. They saw Stalin as history's tool, the instrument of communism's "dictatorship of the proletariat" phase. His economic policies (abandoning the NEP, state control by nationalization and Five-Year Plans, the collectivization of agriculture) supported this argument well. So too, perhaps, does his ruthless liquidation of "bourgeois" elements in the state, such as kulaks and ex-Mensheviks.

Betrayer of the Revolution?

Other Marxists, following in Trotsky's footsteps, admit that Stalin's economics were within the mainstream of communist development but believe that politically and socially he betrayed the Revolution. Aspects of his rule that appeared distinctly uncommunist included the development of his own personality cult, the accumulation of power into the hands of one man, and his fostering of nationalism.

"On the Leninist Path to Communism." This Soviet propaganda poster depicts a youthful Stalin, against a background of technological progress, as the wise father of his people guiding them toward a prosperous communist future.

Most Bolshevik leaders were educated internationalists who believed that in Russia they were paving the way for communist revolutions elsewhere. Stalin, on the other hand, was an out-and-out nationalist. Despite his protests to the contrary, his "Socialism in one country" linked the heritage of the Revolution to Russian nationalism. This denied communism's original international perspective. It is worth pointing out, however, that although this was a setback for communism, it may not have been for Russia. Stalin made his compatriots feel proud of their unique contribution to world history, and the nationalism he created helped them triumph in the Great Patriotic War.

"Higher and Higher"—by the latter 20th century, few Soviet citizens were able to take seriously their leadership's simplistic propaganda.

Child of the Revolution?

Non-Marxist historians side with Stalin's critics. They compare unfavorably his unbending attitude to Lenin's comparative flexibility (over economic policy, for example). While admitting that the democratic ideals of the 1917 Revolution were in tatters by 1924, they believe Stalin took the process much further, refashioning the Revolution in his own image and to his own glory. Privately, he saw himself not as Lenin's successor but more in the tradition of a hero-tsar like Ivan the Terrible, Peter the Great, or Alexander I. When congratulated on the Red Army's reaching Berlin in 1945, he replied with a touch of jealous regret that in 1814, Alexander I had reached Paris.

It may also be argued, however, that Stalin was less the betrayer of the Revolution than its inevitable outcome. This accepts Lord Acton's famous dictum in a letter to Bishop Crighton in 1887:

 Power tends to corrupt, and absolute power corrupts absolutely. Great men are almost always bad men.

In other words, Stalin's monolithic tyranny was simply his version of what Lenin and his colleagues had created to secure communism within the USSR.

THE FINAL LEGACY

The Legacy Secure?

In 1953, the legacy of the Revolution looked secure. In contrast to the tsarist armies of 1914–1917, the Red Army had emerged triumphant during the Great Patriotic War. Eight years later, the Soviet Union was developing technology that would enable it to launch the first Earth-orbiting satellite (1957) and put the first man in space (1961). Its revamped security service, the KGB (1954), eliminated internal opposition. Nuclear weapons and a buffer zone of Soviet-dominated communist satellite states in Eastern Europe protected the USSR from external threats.

The successful establishment of communist regimes in Eastern Europe, North Korea, and China (1949) indicated that communism could be successfully exported. Furthermore, there were many in both the developed and developing worlds (particularly the European colonies) who saw it as an attractive alternative to Western capitalism and imperialism. This gave Soviet power a certain moral authority, particularly when, in 1956, Stalin's successor, Nikita Khruschev (First Secretary of the Central Committee of the Communist Party, 1953–1964), openly denounced his predecessor's cruel excesses.

Nikita Khruschev, the Soviet leader who denounced Stalinist tyranny but was unable to find a communist way of matching the West's remarkable economic expansion after World War II.

Flaws in the System

Following the collapse of the USSR in 1991, it is now clear that the Soviet system was seriously flawed. First, its political structure lacked flexibility and the ability to initiate change. In rejecting both Stalinism and the collective leadership of the Politburo, Khruschev found himself increasingly isolated and was removed from power in 1964. Leonid Brezhnev (First Secretary of the Soviet Communist Party, 1964–1982), Yuri Andropov (1982–1984), and Konstantin Chernenko (1984–1985) drew their authority from consensus. This meant trying to win over all powerful groups (especially the military) and hiding inactivity behind a mask of stability.

Second, the state-controlled Soviet economy, hampered by bureaucracy and rigid controls, could not compete with the booming capitalist economies in the post-war world. As the USSR lagged further and further behind in technology and consumer goods, popular discontent mounted.

Security through strength?
Soviet missiles being paraded
through Red Square, Moscow,
in 1965.

The Military Factor

A third weakness in the Soviet system was the disproportionate power wielded by the military. Politicians were unable to deny demands for military expenditure required by the Cold War. This distorted the Soviet economy and reduced investment in new non-military assets and technology. Pressure from the military also involved the Soviet Union in costly and degrading foreign escapades, such as the invasion of Afghanistan.

Finally, the Soviets found they could maintain control over Eastern Europe only by military might. This led to widely condemned invasions of Hungary (1956) and Czechoslovakia (1968). Ten years later, an unsuccessful war in Afghanistan (1979–1989) revealed serious shortcomings within the Red Army. By 1985, it was clear to most observers that the aims of the 1917 Revolution needed to be rethought, if they were to survive. Chernenko's successor, Mikhail Gorbachev (b. 1931), felt a rethinking of the Soviet position was:

We will be obeyed! Soviet
tanks snuff out the liberal
"Prague Spring" of 1968.

...an urgent necessity arising from the profound processes of the development in our socialist society. This society is ripe for change.

Gorbachev's Plan

Gorbachev's early career is evidence of the better side of the revolutionary legacy. Born into a peasant family, his intelligence was recognized by the local Party that sponsored his education at Moscow University, from which he graduated with distinction in 1955. After joining the Politburo in 1979, he became Party leader and effective head of state in 1985.

Gorbachev realized that the Soviet system was heading for economic disaster. He responded with a three-pronged reform plan: *détente* (more friendly relations with the West), *Perestroika* ("restructuring" of the Communist Party, the economy, and society), and *Glasnost* ("openness" to debate and new ideas).

Détente in action: a meeting between Premier Gorbachev and British Prime Minister Margaret Thatcher in 1989. Gorbachev's policies earned him far greater admiration abroad than within the Soviet Union.

Reform from Within

Of the three policies, *détente* was the most successful. Gorbachev's frequent meetings with Western leaders significantly eased East–West tension and earned him much respect outside the USSR. *Perestroika* and *Glasnost*, however, proved disastrous. Gorbachev's mistake was to try to modify radically the Soviet system from within and yet leave it essentially intact. In so doing, he opened a Pandora's box of troubles, raising expectations that could not be met and alienating both traditionalists and radicals.

Perestroika, for example, involved promoting within the Party radical reformers like the mayor of Moscow, Boris Yeltsin (b. 1931), who wished to go further than Gorbachev toward a Western-style democracy and free-market economy. Cuts in subsidies designed to make the economy more efficient produced shortages and

Boris the savior! Boris Yeltsin, Russia's first freely elected president, addressing crowds of his supporters in August 1991.

hardship. Meanwhile, *Glasnost's* relaxation of censorship meant that the media were flooded with years of pent-up complaints. Most significant was the call from the Soviet nationalities and satellite states of Eastern Europe for full independence from Moscow.

Meltdown

By the end of 1989, popular uprisings had overthrown the communist regimes in the Soviet satellite states of Eastern Europe (see pages 68–69). Within the USSR, open elections to the Supreme Soviet had produced deputies critical of the slow pace of Gorbachev's reforms. In 1990, Yeltsin became chairman of the Supreme Soviet and *de facto* prime minister. Elected president of Russia by a huge majority in the general election of the following year, he clearly stated his disillusionment with communism:

...it was decided to carry out this Marxist experiment on us .... In the end, we proved that there is no place for this idea. It has simply pushed us off the path taken by the world's civilized countries.

The last act in the drama was sparked by an attempted military coup in August 1991. It was thwarted by massive popular opposition, led by Yeltsin, who then outlawed the Communist Party. Gorbachev resigned on Christmas Day, 1991, and seven days later the USSR ceased to exist. With striking irony, the communists had been removed from power by the same force that had handed it to them 74 years earlier: popular discontent.

The breakup of the USSR, 1991.

A Fossilized Relic

Assessment of the Soviet regime has only just started. For the moment, therefore, we will confine ourselves to two questions: Why did Soviet communism collapse when it did, and was the Revolution fatally flawed from the start?

The Soviet Union of the early 1980s was a fossilized relic of a bygone era. Its leaders—Brezhnev, Andropov, and Chernenko—had cut their political teeth under Stalinism and retained the suspicions and fears of that dreadful era. The state's principal institutions—the Communist Party and the military—were primarily concerned with keeping things as they were: Change, which only they could initiate, would inevitably involve their losing power, position, and wealth.

A New World

Gorbachev recognized the need for change but chose to act through the Party rather than with popular backing. Moreover, once he had relaxed the repressive forces that had held people in check since the Revolution, the situation reverted to something similar to 1917: Crowds of dissatisfied workers in the streets calling for a new government. In 1917, the call had been for socialism; in 1990–1991, the watchword was free-market liberal democracy.

Forced labor, communist-style: a scene in a labor camp (*gulag*) in Soviet Central Asia, 1947.

The outside world had moved on. In the 1920s, the Soviet government had not seemed too bad after the miseries of incompetent tsarism and foreign and civil war; during the 1930s, communism had at least sheltered the USSR's citizens from capitalism's Great Depression; and in the 1940s and early 1950s, the regime basked in the glory of victory and conquest. Thirty years later, however, its reason for being was gone. Looking out from their drab apartments behind the Iron Curtain, citizens of the Soviet bloc saw the booming West as a promised land denied to them by bigoted old men who were dedicated to the institutions of the past. When Gorbachev finally gave his people a chance to express their discontent, they did so with a will that surprised even themselves.

Rule by old men wedded to an inflexible, outdated ideology: the Soviet Politburo, 1982. Front row (left to right): Andrei Gromyko, Viktor Grishin, Konstantin Chernenko, Leonid Brezhnev, Arvid Pelshe, Nikolai Tikhonov.

A Doomed Experiment?

Was the regime established in 1917–1922 doomed to failure? Ultimately, as with all historical "if onlys," the question cannot be answered. However, we can suggest features that made such an outcome likely. First, it was an imposed political system that betrayed and then denied the popular will. In the era of mass communication and international media power, no such regime has been able to maintain itself for long. Second, by concentrating power in a few unrepresentative hands and binding itself to a single political dogma (Marxism), it found it hard to adapt to changing needs and situations. Third, in the long run its centrally directed economic system was unable to match the performance of the free market.

With hindsight these flaws are only too apparent. As late as 1988, however, U.S. presidential candidate George Bush had declared,

> *I think the jury is still out on the Soviet experiment.*

Yet only two years later, it had reached its unanimous verdict.

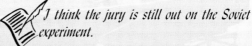
Women at a Moscow bus stop, 1955. Compared with the more prosperous West, life in Soviet Russia was drab, dreary, and restricted.

COMMUNISM BETWEEN THE WARS

Communism in the West to 1939

The first practical effect of the Revolution outside Russia was to alter the strategic balance in World War I. However, Russia's withdrawal from the conflict was soon counterbalanced by the build-up of U.S. forces on the western front. After the failure of the German Spring Offensive in 1918, the Central Powers' brief advantage had been overcome.

Away from the battlefields, the Revolution had an enormous impact on left-wing politics. Before the 1914–1918 war, most Marxist-inclined parties had shunned revolution in favor of achieving socialism through the democratic process. Democratic socialists had regarded Russian revolutionaries as somewhat strange and unrealistic.

Communist Parties

The success of the Bolshevik Revolution forced socialists everywhere to completely rethink their position. Guided by Comintern, more extreme left-wingers broke with their moderate colleagues to set up Bolshevik-style communist parties in most major Western states, including Germany (1919), France (1920), Spain (1920), and Italy (1921). A Communist Party was even established in the United States (1919).

Revolutionary communism made little headway in the "Anglo-Saxon" democracies. In the United States it reached a peak of popularity in the 1932 presidential election, when the communist candidate polled 103,000 votes. In Britain, the Communist Party failed to make headway against the nonrevolutionary socialist Labour Party.

Communism and Fascism

Elsewhere, communist parties played more important

"Down with fascism"—a communist poster from the Spanish Civil War of 1936–1939, the first major European conflict involving communists since the Russian Revolution.

roles. In 1934, after years of squabbling among groups, the French Communist Party allied with the Socialists in the face of the fascist threat and won 16 percent of the seats in the National Assembly. Similarly, the Spanish communists were at their strongest when operating within the Popular Front, opposed to Franco's right-wing regime, during the Spanish Civil War (1936–1939).

In Italy and Germany, fear of communism played an important part in the rise of fascism. One reason why Mussolini's coup of 1922 was successful was that to frightened conservatives *il Duce* offered a defense against left-wing radicalism, spearheaded by the communists. Four years later, Mussolini exiled or imprisoned the communist leadership.

The German communists, whose Spartakist group had launched an unsuccessful coup in 1919, gained widespread support during the early years of the Great Depression. In the 1932 Reichstag elections, they polled almost six million votes. Popular acceptance of the Nazis was partly a reaction to this communist upsurge. In 1932, Adolf Hitler declared,

Yes, we have formed the inexorable decision to destroy Marxism in Germany, down to its very last root.

On coming to power in 1933, Hitler swiftly and forcibly eliminated the communists and other left-wing parties. Therefore, despite its popularity immediately after World War I and during the early years of the Great Depression, communism failed to establish itself as the basis for government outside the USSR. Furthermore, its most notable European legacy was precisely the opposite: the emergence of totalitarian regimes in Italy, Germany, and Spain dedicated to its elimination.

The monster born of the fear of communism—a Nazi rally, 1935.

Marxism–Leninism

Marxism was founded on the belief that a communist revolution would occur only in industrial countries controlled by bourgeois elites. This had, by definition, little appeal beyond Western Europe and the United States. Lenin, seeking to adapt Marxism to the situation within tsarist Russia, incorporated the concept of imperialism into the original philosophy. He claimed that by expanding their markets into nonindustrialized colonies and sharing some of their profits with a "labor aristocracy," the imperialist bourgeoisie divided the proletariat and so made worldwide revolution impossible without the leadership of "professional revolutionaries."

The apparent triumph of Lenin's thesis in Russia gave Marxism a new relevance to the masses in the colonies of the imperialist powers and to the peasant classes in nonindustrialized countries. Marxism (or, strictly speaking, Marxism–Leninism) was no longer a message of hope solely to the toiling urban proletariat of the West, but to exploited workers everywhere. Consequently, between the world wars, influential communist parties emerged in India, Indo-China, Indonesia, South Africa, several countries in Latin America, Cuba, and, most significant of all, China. In those countries under European rule (notably Indonesia and Vietnam), the communists, urged on by Moscow, were generally prominent in independence movements.

Communism in China

Interestingly, it was not in a colonial country but in one of the world's oldest independent nations—China—that communism made the greatest advance outside the USSR before 1939. Founded in 1921, the Chinese Communist Party (CCP) found itself obliged by Comintern to ally with another supposedly Leninist party, the Guomindang (KMT). In 1925, leadership of the KMT passed to General Chiang Kai-shek. After taking control of most of the country, in 1927 Chiang renounced his links with Moscow and set about trying to destroy the CCP. This proved more difficult than he had anticipated.

By 1931, the CCP was firmly established around the Jianxi Soviet. It boasted around 300,000 members, an effective Red Army, and a centralized leadership. Ominously for Moscow,

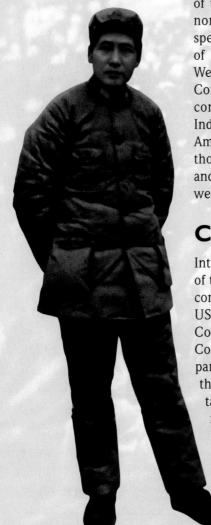

Hero-chairman in waiting – the future Chinese leader Mao Tse-tung in the 1930s.

Mao Tse-tung on the Long March, 1934. The communists heralded their "March" (or ride, for Mao) as an epoch-making victory over the capitalist-backed KMT.

its rising star, Mao Tse-tung, was beginning to fashion a distinctive Chinese form of communism (Maoism). This emphasized local initiatives, the importance of the non-industrialized peasantry, and the need for each generation to rediscover revolutionary zeal.

In 1934–1935, the Chinese communists escaped the advancing KMT forces by undertaking an epic "Long March." Mao, a master of propaganda, optimistically (but correctly) prophesized that the march would prove a victory of considerable significance:

 The Long March is also a seeding-machine. In the eleven provinces it has sown many seeds which will sprout, leaf, blossom, and bear fruit, and will yield a harvest in the future.

For the time being, though, Mao's harvest had to wait. In 1937, Japanese forces launched an invasion of China, and the CCP and KMT reluctantly formed a united front against their common enemy.

Limited Success

The world situation during the 1920s and 1930s—the postwar slump, the Great Depression, and growing colonial revolt—appeared ideally suited to the spread of Soviet-style communism. It was even advocated by the American Writers Congress, which declared in 1935:

Communism must come and must be fought for.

And yet, as we have seen, although Moscow-backed communist parties sprang up all over the globe, nowhere in this period did they repeat the Bolshevik success of 1917.

Obviously, the communists' failure to take power in any individual country depended upon specific conditions there. The British Communist Party's failure to make much impact, for example, was largely due to the working class' deep attachment to a Labour Party wedded to a peaceful and democratic revolution rather than a violent one. Nonetheless, specifics aside, several general points can be made about communism's limited expansion before 1945.

The Tarnished Image

First, the romantic image of the Bolsheviks fostered by themselves and foreign commentators such as John Reed was soon tarnished when their brutality and intolerance became apparent. By the time of Stalin's dictatorship, communism was widely associated with tyranny and brutality. Stalin's unwillingness to strive to extend the Soviet system—shown by his "Socialism in one country" policy—further limited communism's prospects.

Second, the conditions that the Bolsheviks had used so skillfully—the power vacuum created by defeat, a breakdown in law and order, and mass discontent of all classes with the existing regime—were never precisely repeated elsewhere.

A desolate scene from the depression in Britain in the 1930s. Although mass unemployment might have provided a fertile ground for communism, it made little headway among the poverty-stricken working class.

LINE FOR RESTAURANT
20 MEALS FOR 18
DONATIONS INVITED
HELP FEED THE HUNGRY
I WILL FEED 20
RESTAURANT
107 W 43rd ST.

Unemployed Americans line up for bread during the Great Depression.

Communist literature considered subversive was seized in Boston in November 1919.

Significantly, in Germany and China, where there was some similarity with the Russian situation, the communists attracted a considerable following.

Anti-Communism

Third, communism was to some extent a victim of its own success. Now that they had seen that a communist revolution was not just a dream, anti-communists of all persuasions (from democratic socialists to conservatives and imperialists) took steps to ensure that it would not reoccur. Continual anti-communist propaganda was one of the measures employed. A well-known example is the forged letter published in the right-wing British press in 1924, supposedly from Zinoviev, head of Comintern, urging revolutionary activity in Britain. Typical of many "Reds under the bed" scares of the time, it helped in the defeat of the Labour government (which had recognized the USSR) in the subsequent election. Anti-communists also introduced measures intended to lessen working-class alienation, improve conditions for the poor, and strengthen democracy. These included making the vote available to more people (often including women), better social security, and higher taxes for the wealthy.

Finally, the advance of communism was stemmed by the emergence of fervently anti-communist parties and movements that played on nationalist sentiments. Among the better known are the fascist parties of Italy and Germany, Franco's Falange, Chiang Kai-shek's KMT, and the New State of President Vargas of Brazil.

RISE AND FALL

A Potent Legacy

World War II left the USSR in a position of power and influence. By fighting alongside the Western Allies, it had come in from the diplomatic cold. Its forces were widely respected. In 1945, the Soviets occupied a sweep of territories around the USSR's borders, including Poland, East Germany, Czechoslovakia, Hungary, Romania, Bulgaria, Mongolia, and North Korea. Pro-Soviet regimes were establishing themselves in Yugoslavia and Albania.

Furthermore, in a world devastated by war, the communist gospel of hope for the homeless, jobless, and oppressed found eager listeners. From China and Vietnam in the East to Greece in the West, the Red Star was in the ascendancy. By 1949, when Mao's communists had vanquished the KMT and established the communist People's Republic of China, and communist governments had been established throughout Eastern Europe, the legacy of 1917 had never looked more powerful.

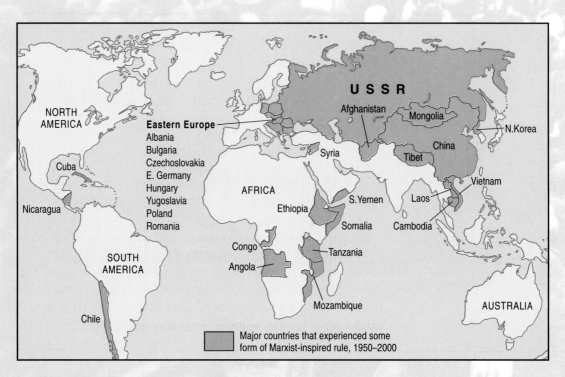

USSR

Afghanistan   Mongolia

NORTH
AMERICA   **Eastern Europe**   N.Korea
                         Albania
                         Bulgaria   China
                         Czechoslovakia   Syria   Tibet
Cuba   E. Germany
                         Hungary   AFRICA   Vietnam
                         Yugoslavia   S.Yemen   Laos
Nicaragua   Poland   Ethiopia
                         Romania   Somalia   Cambodia

                                         Congo
                                                       Tanzania
                         SOUTH   Angola
                         AMERICA

                                         Mozambique
                                                                              AUSTRALIA
         Chile

         Major countries that experienced some
         form of Marxist-inspired rule, 1950–2000

The closest the world has come to nuclear destruction— newspaper headlines at the time of the U.S.–Soviet Cuban Missile Crisis, 1962.

Cold War

Within this success lay the seeds of Soviet communism's downfall. The USSR was not the only country brought out of relative isolation by World War II. By 1947, the United States, the world's undisputed economic and technological giant, was determined to act as worldwide champion of capitalist democracy. So the scene was set for 45 years of capitalist–communist rivalry, known as the Cold War.

The Cold War was Soviet communism's undoing. Had the USSR returned to its 1930s policy of "Socialism in one country," it might still exist today. However, two factors made this impossible. First, the USSR had a wall of puppet states to control and defend. Second, its apparent aggression in the postwar years (which was, in fact, largely driven by fear of the West) spurred American administrations to seek to destroy the "evil empire" by any measures short of full-scale war. Indeed, some Americans were not prepared to accept even that limit. General Thomas Power, commander of the U.S. Strategic Air Command in the 1960s, said,

 The whole idea is to kill the[m]. At the end of the war, if there are two Americans and one Russian left alive, we win.

An Old Story

The Cold War had arrived when Winston Churchill declared publicly in 1946 that an "iron curtain" had descended across Europe, dividing East from West. Tensions rose during the USSR's blockade of West Berlin (isolated within East Germany) in 1948–1949. When Stalin's North Korean allies invaded U.S.-backed South Korea, it flared into a 3-year "hot" war (1950–1953).

Over the next 25 years, the USSR sought to combat capitalist democracy and boost communism by supplying arms, aid, and, occasionally, by direct military intervention. In Vietnam and Cuba it met with success. In other areas, most notably in Afghanistan and several newly independent African countries, high-handed Soviet tactics too often alienated the bulk of the population by bolstering unpopular regimes. Time and again, it was the story of 1917–1924 retold: tyranny stalking in beneath the banner of freedom.

Rumbles of Discontent

Though some countries (Czechoslovakia in 1948, for example) appeared to have freely chosen a communist government, once in power the communists were there to stay. Marxist theory supported this position—since communism was the highest form of government, free elections were unnecessary. Too often, though, such rhetoric masked the determination of a Moscow-backed elite to cling to power.

The Hungarians were the first to attempt to break the mold. In 1956, after Imre Nagy's moderate, anti-Soviet government had withdrawn Hungary from the Warsaw Pact (the communist military alliance formed in May 1955), 150,000 Pact troops invaded the country and forcibly restored hard-line communism. Similarly, when the Czech leader Alexander Dubcek introduced a more relaxed form of communism into his country in 1968, Warsaw Pact forces again intervened to stamp out destabilizing dissidence. This was the intolerant legacy of the Bolsheviks within the Soviet Bloc.

A statue of Stalin lies abandoned in a Budapest street during the Hungarian anti-Soviet uprising of 1956.

"The Atheist"—a Soviet propaganda cartoon showing an honest communist perplexed by Christian doctrine. In fact, communism itself was a kind of religion, offering explanation of the present and hope for the future.

Communism and Religion

Serious dissent next flared in Poland, in 1980. In the hands of militant trade union leaders like Lech Walesa, demonstrations against price rises turned into full-scale political opposition. Although the Polish government declared martial law and banned trade unionism, the opposition smoldered on. It was nourished by the Roman Catholic Church, whose leader, Pope John Paul II, was himself a Pole.

Communism had always held religion in contempt for being "unscientific" and directing people toward heavenly rather than earthly goals. This hostility helps explain why communism failed to capture the hearts of the fervently Catholic Poles. In 1980, for example, Walesa said of the influence of Soviet communism in Poland:

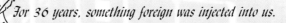

For 36 years, something foreign was injected into us.

Communism's dismissive attitude toward religion also explains why it never took deep root in staunchly Muslim countries.

Division and Retreat

While the peoples of Eastern Europe merely tolerated their Moscow-backed masters, Soviet communism was being undermined from an unexpected quarter. By the late 1950s, rifts were appearing between China and the USSR. In 1958–1960, the two split and proceeded along different paths. Communism's inability to present the world with a united front damaged its international image. The rift widened when, following Mao's death in 1976, Deng Xiaoping introduced into China a number of economic reforms based on free-market, capitalist principles.

By the late 1980s, therefore, the communism of Eastern Europe, maintained by Soviet force, looked increasingly out of place. When Gorbachev introduced *Glasnost* and *Perestroika* (see page 56) and the Eastern European leaders were reluctant to follow his lead, the people took matters into their own hands. Deprived of Soviet military backing, one by one the communist regimes crumbled in the face of popular uprisings. Poland established a democratic government in August 1989, and within two years communist government was just a memory throughout Eastern Europe.

Lech Walesa, the leader of the Polish Solidarity trade union, was a symbol of his country's resistance to Soviet authority. He was elected president of Poland in 1990.

The dream lives on—members of communist Cuba's Young Workers' Army, 1996.

The Great Failure?

By the end of the 20th century, the gradual introduction of free-market economics into China left Cuba as the only remaining old-style Marxist state.

The collapse of communism was greeted with widespread rejoicing. Nonetheless, there was a tinge of sadness behind the partying. As one East German told a BBC reporter in 1990:

Yes, I think we will be richer. And we will be more free, too. But still I think we have lost something. The old ways were corrupt, but our dream was not corrupt. Now it is each man for himself. Then there was a feeling—buried deep, of course—that we acted not for ourselves but for the common good.

A Gloomy Prognosis

These remarks expressed the disappointment in some circles that a great experiment—perhaps the greatest political experiment ever undertaken—had failed. A utopian world in which wealth was distributed "from each according to his ability, to each according to his needs" appeared unattainable. The ultimate blame, it seemed, lay not with Marxism but with human nature.

Perhaps, as Christian teachers had preached for centuries, we are a fallen species. Since we are driven primarily by self-interest, the only enduring form of government appears to be one that balances the self-seeking of one group with that of another.

Lessons Learned...

That said, the legacy of 1917 did not vanish altogether. It endured, after a fashion, in China. Elsewhere, strangely, it survived in the measures put in place to make further communist revolution unlikely: equality of opportunity, social security, full adult suffrage, universal education, and moderate redistribution of wealth.

Nor was Marxist analysis entirely set aside, either. No one can now write history without taking class and economic forces into careful consideration. Moreover, in the late 1990s, protestors disrupted meetings of international financial summits. The violent riots that greeted the World Trade Organization talks in Seattle in 1999, and in Genoa, Italy, in 2001, showed that anti-capitalist sentiment was by no means a spent force.

...and Not Learned

Despite such protest, free-market capitalism now appears triumphant everywhere. However, the system cannot go on expanding forever. When it finally runs out of steam, an alternative, more sustainable way of life will be sought. Nor can the gap between rich nations and poor continue to grow without the latter forcibly attempting to improve the situation. It is possible, therefore, that at some point the old dogmas of 1917 will be taken down, dusted, adapted, and put forth again.

Shades of Petrograd, 1917? Anti-capitalist protestors at the meeting of the World Trade Organization, Seattle, 1999.

Marxism

Marxism grew from two roots. One, as old as human history, was the feeling that it was wrong for the few to enjoy great wealth while the masses lived in poverty. The second, which enjoyed a widespread following during the 19th century, was the belief that science held the key to understanding everything about the world. The German philosopher Karl Marx (1818–1883), assisted by Friedrich Engels (1820–1895), combined the two to produce a "scientific" philosophy of history.

Marxism, which received its most detailed exposition in Marx's three-volume *Das Kapital* (1867 onward), claimed to explain the fundamental laws of history. Driven in the last instance by economic forces, human society progressed in three fundamental stages: feudal, capitalist (the one industrialized countries were in at the time he was writing), and communist. In communist societies, all wealth was supposed to be held in common and nation states were expected to wither away.

The capitalist stage was marked by the exploitation of workers—paying them less than the value of their labor. This stage would end when the workers, the real producers of wealth, rose in revolution. The final stage of human development—communism—would then supposedly emerge after a period of "dictatorship of the proletariat," during which selfish capitalist (or bourgeois) habits and thinking would be eliminated.

The great strength of Marx's philosophy was its explanation of the misery of the time as well as its offering of possible hope for the future. However, Marxism was betrayed by its practitioners, who used it as a means of establishing control over the mass of workers and peasants and subjecting other classes of entrepreneurs and bourgeoisie to extinction or imprisonment.

The German philosopher Karl Marx, upon whose writings the entire edifice of modern communism was based.

GLOSSARY

Abdicate to surrender the throne voluntarily

Autocracy absolute, unquestionable rule by a single divinely appointed ruler

Autonomy the right and ability to act independently

Bolsheviks section of the divided SD party led by Lenin (literally, "the majority")

Bourgeoisie middle or capitalist class

Bureaucracy civil service or other system of administration

Capitalist Marxist term for the free-market economy driven by competition and the quest for profit; to the radical left, "capitalist" is a term of abuse

Central Powers alliance of Germany and Austria–Hungary during World War I

Coalition government made up of more than one party

Communist society in which all goods and wealth are held in common; modern communism follows the teachings of Marx (see page 72) and the variations of Lenin and Mao Tse-tung; also the name adopted by the Bolsheviks in 1918

Conservative opposed to change; usually anti-left

Coup forcible change of government

Defeatist position of revolutionaries who denounced World War I as an imperialist–capitalist venture and were therefore not prepared to fight

Defensism position taken by revolutionaries who, while not approving of World War I, were prepared to defend Russia from enemy aggression

Democracy popular government; both liberals (who emphasize government by the people) and communists (who emphasize government for the people) claim to be democrats

Duma Russian parliament set up after the 1905 Revolution

Emancipation setting free (from serfdom or other oppression)

Factionalism group within a government with self-seeking aims

Fascism right-wing, totalitarian political movement that emphasized nationalism and the cult of the leader

Federal having power divided between central and regional or local governments

Feudalism economic and social system prevalent in Europe during the Middle Ages, based on the exchange of land (the primary source of wealth) for service; the bulk of the population was landless peasants, or serfs

Franchise right to vote

Imperialist seeking or having an empire. Lenin believed imperialism was an offshoot of capitalism

Intelligentsia class of highly educated scholars, writers, and thinkers

Kadet Russia's liberal Constitutional Democratic Party

Left inclined to socialist or communist views

Liberal political position that emphasizes individual freedom and rights

Marxism–Leninism Marx's teachings, as adapted by Lenin (see page 62)

Marxist following the teachings of Karl Marx (see page 72)

Mensheviks branch of the SDs that split with Lenin's Bolsheviks (literally, "the minority")

Mir village commune

Peasant small-scale farmer

Proletariat Marxist name for the urban working class

Purge remove or clear out political opponents, usually by force

Reformation period of religious, political, and social upheaval in Europe (16th and 17th centuries) when the Christian Church divided between Roman Catholicism and Protestantism

Republic state without a monarch

Right inclined toward conservatism

SDs Marxist revolutionary Social Democratic Party of the early 20th century that split between Bolsheviks and Mensheviks

Serfdom condition in which unfree poor farmers worked land owned by a noble class that also had other legal rights over them

Socialist confusing term that embraces a wide range of left-wing political positions, both revolutionary (communist) and nonrevolutionary

Soviet communist council of deputies. Also used as an adjective form of "USSR," as in the "Soviet government"

SRs Socialist Revolutionary Party that wanted a democratic, federal Russia and the common ownership of land

Totalitarian intolerant rule by one party, small group, or single leader

Tsar emperor; title of Russia's hereditary ruler

Tsarevitch heir to the Russian throne; a tsar's eldest son

Tsaritsa empress; the tsar's wife

Unilateral decision or action of one side only

USSR Union of Soviet Socialist Republics, the Russian-dominated confederation of communist republics that replaced the Russian Empire

Zemstva local councils (singular = *zemstvo*), replaced by soviets after 1917

TIMELINE OF EVENTS

1881–1894	Reign of Alexander III	
1892	Witte becomes minister of finance	
1894–1917	Reign of Nicholas II	
1902	SRs founded	
1903	SDs split between Bolsheviks and Mensheviks	
1904–1905	Russo–Japanese War	
1905	1905 Revolution	
1906	First Duma meets	
1906–1911	Stolypin's reforms	
1912	Lena Goldfields massacre	
1914	Outbreak of World War I	
1915	Nicholas II becomes commander-in-chief	
1917 Feb.	Revolution in Petrograd; Petrograd Soviet formed	
March	Provisional Government formed; Nicholas II abdicates	
June	Military offensive (to July)	
July	"July Days"; Kerensky becomes minister-president	
Aug.	Kornilov coup fails	
Sept.	Trotsky chair of Petrograd Soviet	
Oct.	Bolshevik coup in Petrograd	
Nov.	Bolshevik power extends to Moscow; elections to Constituent Assembly	
Dec.	Armistice	
1918 Jan.	Constituent Assembly forcibly closed	
Mar.	Treaty of Brest-Litovsk;	

Civil War (to 1922); Bolsheviks become Communist Party; Cheka formed; War Communism introduced

1921	New Economic Policy
1922	Stalin becomes Communist Party Secretary
1923	USSR established
1924	Death of Lenin
1928	Stalin supreme in USSR (to 1953); first Five-Year Plan (collectivization of agriculture)
1936–1938	Stalin's purges
1939	Nazi–Soviet Pact; outbreak of World War II in Europe
1941	Nazi invasion of the USSR; start of the Great Patriotic War (to 1945)
1945	Red Army enters Berlin
1945–1948	Communist governments set up in Eastern Europe
1946	Cold War begins
1949	Communists come to power in China
1958–1960	Sino–Soviet split
1985	Gorbachev General Secretary of the Communist Party
1989–1990	Communist governments swept away in Eastern Europe
1991	Yeltsin elected President of Russia; USSR ceases to exist

BOOKS TO READ

Edwards, Judith. *Lenin and the Russian Revolution in World History (In World History)*. Berkeley Heights, NJ: Enslow Publishers Inc., 2001.

Gilbert, Adrian. *The Russian Revolution*. New York: Raintree Steck-Vaughn, 1996.

Kallan, Stuart A. *Before the Communist Revolution: Russian History Through 1919*. Minneapolis, MN: Abdo Publishing, 1992.

Vail, John J. *"Peace, Land, Bread!": A History of the Russian Revolution (World History Library)*. New York: Facts on File Inc., 1996.

Willoughby, Susan. *The Russian Revolution*. Chicago, IL: Heinemann Library, 1998.

INDEX